BRITAIN IN OLD PHOTOGRAPHS

FLEET

PERCY VICKERY

SUTTON PUBLISHING LIMITED

Sutton Publishing Limited
Phoenix Mill · Thrupp · Stroud
Gloucestershire · GL5 2BU

First published 1998

Reprinted 1999

Copyright © Percy Vickery, 1998

Cover photographs, front: Mr E. Field's shop,
1927; *back*: Terrace Garage, 1933.

British Library Cataloguing in Publication Data
A catalogue record for this book is available from the
British Library.

ISBN 0-7509-1901-9

Typeset in 10/12 Perpetua.
Typesetting and origination by
Sutton Publishing Limited.
Printed in Great Britain by
Ebenezer Baylis, Worcester.

Crested china. These souvenirs were available in most towns and cities from the 1890s until the Second
World War. They can be found in any shape or subject with a local, county, regimental or personal coat of
arms. A variety of manufacturers including Goss, Florentine, Grafton and Arcadian produced an amazing
range. The origin of the three fir trees as Fleet's coat of arms is a mystery as the earliest known local use
of this device is in the Chamber of Trade journals of the 1920s, but much of this china is of an earlier
period. The crests vary slightly between manufacturers. No Crookham pieces are known but 'The
Calthorpe Arms, Elvetham' has been seen.

CONTENTS

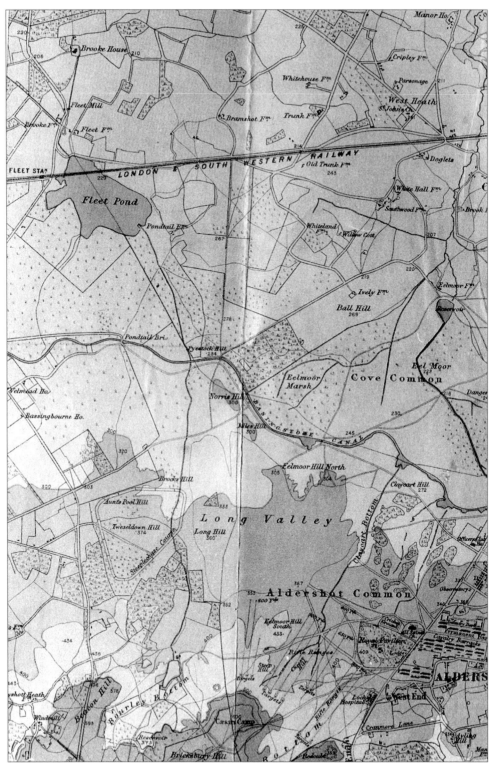

A map of Fleet area in about 1865, showing the railway, canal and pond with a few houses and farms.

INTRODUCTION

Fleet, originally in the Hundred of Crondall, was in the Tithing of Crookham and probably derived its name from the 130 acre pond at the north end of the town, which in ancient times was known as Flete. The pond, the largest in Hampshire, was an important fishery in medieval times and was made Crown property when the army came to Aldershot in 1854. The pond became a Nature Reserve in 1972 when the large pond and surrounding area was bought by Fleet Council.

In 1505 the fishery of Fleet (the pond) and the pasture of Le Flete were leased by the Prior and Convent of St Swithin, Winchester, at a rent of 'a hundred fishes for the fishery and 23/4 [£1 3s 4d] for the pasture'; the fish were to be delivered to the priory at Winchester in good condition in Lent or between Easter and Pentecost. In 1536 a similar lease was granted for sixty years to start at the expiration of the original thirty year lease, but now instead of sending fish to Winchester a rent of 20s per annum was charged. In 1567 a 'Great Storm' caused the banks of the northern pond to be washed away and the pond drained; this left the other pond retained by the causeway (now Cove Road). To save expense, Winchester agreed that the banks need not be repaired.

The coming of the London to Southampton Railway Co. in 1847 when Fleet Pond station was opened was to have a great effect on the area, with many hundreds coming down from London to enjoy the beautiful countryside with its heather, rhododendrons and health-giving pines. In the 1850s Fleet pond was attracting crowds of naturalists who came to study the wild flowers which abounded; alas, the rarer species have long since disappeared. In the winter when the pond was invariably frozen over for several weeks special trains came from London to enable skaters to enjoy the facilities. Curling and ice hockey were also popular, with picnics being held on the islands.

Crookham Common, part of the Great Heath, was enclosed in 1834. This was the area which today is Fleet and Church Crookham down to the south and west sides of the pond. This enabled the gentry to split the area to please themselves and a few houses were built to the north of Fleet Road and along Reading Road; by 1875 the population of Fleet was less than 400.

After the Crimean War it was decided to build a hutted camp at Aldershot for 40,000 soldiers together with 25,000 acres on which to carry out training, and this land forms all of the southern boundary of Fleet and Church Crookham. In June 1878 Mr Henry Brake, an estate agent, went to an auction in Farnborough and for £2,210 he bought almost 250 acres of heathland bounded by Fleet and Reading roads, the canal and the pond which Mr Thomas Keep had acquired in 1840 as the result of the Enclosure Act of 1829. The roads were laid out on the American grid system, which was fine in those days but has caused many accidents since the motor car was invented. Public auctions were held in Fleet and London to sell the plots; at the 1882 annual land sale at the Prince of Wales forty-six lots with average frontages of 40 ft were sold at prices from £10 to £70. Crookham village became a parish in 1840 but Fleet and Church Crookham only took that step in 1861. In 1932 the village became a ward of Crondall but Fleet and Church Crookham had already become an Urban District in 1904. After much deliberation the 1974 reorganisation resulted in Hartley Wintney Rural District Council (which included Crookham village) and Fleet Urban District Council amalgamating to become Hart District. Today the population of Fleet and Crookham is 36,000, compared with about 500 in 1871.

One of the early decisions reached when the urban district was formed was to rename four roads to commemorate Queen Victoria's son the Duke of Connaught, who lived locally while GOC Aldershot Command. Later street names commemorated local benefactors and councillors such as Messrs Chinnock, Frere, Wickham, Calthorpe, Oakley, Champion, Johnson, Parsons and Campbell. Many large houses which have been demolished to make way for estates are remembered by road names such as Woodlands, Courtmoor, Stockton, Brinksway, Glebe, Kingscroft, Burnside, Peatmoor, Queen Mary, Stanton, Westbury, Dinorben, Carthonia, Darset and Greenways.

As the population of Fleet and Crookham has grown during the twentieth century so Fleet has moved to various parliamentary constituencies. Originally in the North Hants Division, Aldershot took over in the 1920s where Fleet remained until the 1970s when we were moved to the newly formed East Hampshire seat, only to be moved again when the Boundary Commission created North East Hampshire for the 1997 election. We have at times been represented by Viscount Wolmer, Oliver Lyttleton, Sir Eric Errington, Michael Mates and now James Arbutnot – all Conservatives.

The Aldershot Rural Deanery of which Fleet and Crookham are part were in the Winchester Diocese until 1927 when the new Diocese of Guildford was formed. There were only four parishes on the Hampshire border which moved over to Guildford.

CHAPTER ONE

ORIGINS

Fleet Mill House, 1912. Mrs Mallett, the miller's wife, is standing with their daughters outside their timber-framed and brick dwelling. The internal walls were wattle and daub. The house stood adjacent to the mill, but it is not known if they were built at the same time; the miller was certainly living here in 1800. The house was demolished soon after milling ceased.

Fleet Mill, 1905. Taylor's map of Hampshire (dated 1759) shows that the mill together with half-a-dozen farmhouses were the only buildings on Crookham Common, as Fleet was known at that time. Grain from the surrounding area would be brought in great quantities to the mill to be ground into flour and animal feed. The business continued until about 1940, when all milling ceased. The timber frame was removed by squatters in the 1980s, and the unsafe building was quickly demolished.

Pondtail Bridge and gas holder, 1912. The Aldershot Gas & Water Co. opened an office and showroom close to the station in 1905 when they first brought gas to Fleet. Within a few years a gas holder was built in Velmead Road to store the gas which was produced at Aldershot. In the mid-1970s, when North Sea gas was introduced, the holder became obsolete and was demolished. Houses now stand on the site.

Fleet Weir Bridge, 1908. The Basingstoke Canal was opened in 1794 and linked Basingstoke to the Wey Navigation (a distance of 37 miles) and on to the Thames. Coal, timber, flour, bricks, etc. were carried by the horse-drawn barges. This weir controlled the level of the water, allowing the surplus to be carried along a stream to the pond.

Crookham Swing Bridge, 1906. Situated between Malthouse and Poulters bridges at Zephon Common, it connected the group of cottages beside the bridge to the nearest point in Watery Lane where delivery vehicles could offload. A sack (1 cwt) of coal must have been very heavy to carry from lorry to coal shed (about 400 yards). The canal from Basingstoke to the Greywell Tunnel ceased to be navigable in the 1930s when part of the tunnel roof collapsed.

Mark Hicks. Mark lived for many years at Canal Cottage at Chequers Bridge; the cottage is believed to have been the office of the original company which opened for business in 1794. He was associated with the canal from an early age, some say when he was only ten, and he worked for various owners. When he was in his eighties Mark would work the barge horse when a barge was to be towed for a special occasion. A week before he died he was working as a canal bailiff, and his long service was recorded in the *Guinness Book of Records*.

Mark Hicks' funeral, 1966. Mark was ninety-two when he died, and in his later years his life revolved around the Chequers Inn – where he could be found most evenings recalling incidents from his earlier life for just the price of a pint. His death was marked by one of the last traditional canal funerals. Cecil North is standing in the prow of the barge while Mark's other friends, including Jim Foley and Laurie Winter, head the procession from Crookham Wharf to the coal wharf (between Malthouse and Coxheath bridges). His coffin was then taken to its resting place at Fleet cemetery.

Fleet Pond, *c.* 1910. It is believed that the 130-acre pond was man-made in Roman times; it was apparently in two halves, divided by a causeway which is now Cove Road. In 1567 the 'Great Storm' swept the area and the banks of the northern piece (by the motorway) burst and half the pond drained itself. In 1843 the pond was again divided when the railway was built between Woking and Winchfield.

Elvetham Hall, 1905. Elvetham was owned at the time of the Domesday Book by Chertsey Abbey. It passed into the ownership of the Calthorpe family in 1741 and the family have been Lords of the Manor since then. The estate stretched over Star Hill on the A30, into Winchfield and about 400 yards into what is Fleet today. Except for the railway, which cut the Fleet portion off, it is doubtful whether Calthorpe would have allowed development on his estate. The Golf, Cricket and Rifle clubs were all built on his ground and Fitzroy, Calthorpe and Gough Roads were all named after the 'squire'.

Hop picking, 1922. Hops had been grown in Crookham for at least the last 200 years as the soil was ideal. Three farms were growing the crop and at one time there were four kilns to dry them. The last remaining kiln between the green and Hitches Lane is now a listed building, and is used by several small businesses. In the last century Crookham School often recorded that children arrived late because all the family had been in the fields hop-picking since daybreak.

The White family, 1922. Grove Farm in Crookham village has been the home of the White family since the early 1890s. The 'HH' on the 7-gallon hop basket indicates that it belongs to the Howlings, who owned Cross Farm close to the green. Picking was in September and started at first light when the hops were open with the dew; they were placed in the basket just before the tallyman came along. Payment to the local families was calculated by volume. Picking was not so profitable after about 9 o'clock as the sun dried the hops and they closed up; therefore nearly twice as many were required to fill a basket.

Redfields House, 1896. Built in 1879, the house in Redfield Lane was described as a medium-sized residence standing in 20 acres. Mr Brandon bought the house and surrounding fields in 1896 and produced tobacco from 1912 until 1938. The government's 'Imperial Preference Tax', which favoured Empire growers, killed off the home trade. The house was taken over in 1940 by the War Office and was used as the Officers' Mess for the nearby RAMC Training Centre; ancillary wooden buildings were built in the grounds. The house was empty between 1971 and 1976, when it was bought by PMM as a conference and training centre. When the house again came on the market in 1995 it was bought by St Nicholas' School.

Tobacco plants at Crookham. Mr Brandon grew hops when he first arrived in 1896, but he experimented with tobacco plants until he found one which suited the soil and gave 800 lb of dried leaf to the acre, keeping eight men permanently employed. Several fields near the house were used for the plants, including the site on the corner of Redfields Lane and Ewshot Lane, where the garden centre stands today.

Harvesting tobacco at Crookham. Late summer was the time to harvest the crop; casual labour, mainly women and children, was brought in. Special carts were used as the green leaves had to be hung to prevent bruising. According to quality the leaves were either used to make Blue Pryor cigarettes or Golden Queen pipe tobacco. Some were blended with Empire leaves by H. Stevens of Salisbury to make their brands.

Tobacco drying shed. The drying/curing sheds were opposite Redfields House, where today the industrial estate stands. In the 1960s two large timbered buildings with earth floors still stood at the rear of the site; inside were a series of horizontal timbers at various heights to which the frames of hanging leaves were attached. For its last few years one of the sheds housed spares for obsolete aircraft.

Brook House, 1925. This listed house in the Crondall Road is part of a once-extensive country house with Dutch gables dated 1664. It has a later timber-framed extension. The house has been extensively restored by the present owner. According to local folklore Nell Gwynne visited Charles II here several times. Nearby Two Ponds Cottage is the oldest building in the village, believed to date from the thirteenth or fourteenth century.

Brickfield Cottages, 1918. These four cottages were sited close to the swing bridge a few yards down the lane towards Crookham Village, and no doubt housed workers from the nearby brickworks. Between Ewshot and Crookham there was a seam of clay suitable for making bricks, tiles and pots. While the canal was being constructed there was a brickworks close to Zephon Common which supplied the bricks for the nearby bridges. Brickfield Cottages and another cottage on the towpath were demolished in the 1960s.

Bridge House, 1905. This eighteenth-century house is near Chequers Bridge in the Crondall Road. The grounds were large enough to include Crookham's first cricket ground, and in the 1890s various celebrities brought teams along to challenge the locals. W.G. Grace came on at least one occasion.

The Forge House, 1905. The seventeenth-century house opposite the Black Horse in Crookham Street is a fine timber-framed and brick structure. It is probable that Mr Stevens bought the house and added the forge and ancillary buildings in the mid-nineteenth century. The shoeing, wheelwright and welding business kept Mr Stevens very busy. When Fleet started to grow just before the turn of the century he bought a piece of ground adjacent to the Hart Centre. Business carried on in The Street until the 1950s.

Crookham Road, 1901. Hope Cottages are the nearest houses on this view looking towards the Oatsheaf. Infilling and rebuilding since the 1960s has resulted in smaller gardens and twice as many houses. These houses back on to the canal, some only 6 or 7 ft from the towpath. Lea Lane is about 100 yards along on the left; you could walk a few yards and see cows and pigs at Leawood Farm. Another 100 yards or so after climbing the stile you would be on one of the public footpaths leading out to the quiet Hitches Lane.

Albany Road culvert, 1905. The stream carrying the surplus water from the canal at the weir between Reading Road and Regents Street crosses Albany Road close to the junction with Rochester Grove. During the Second World War a concrete dam was built adjacent to the bridge, enabling a supply of several thousand gallons of water to be retained for fighting fires started in bombing raids. Until the First World War this road from Fleet Road to Kings Road was called Upper Street.

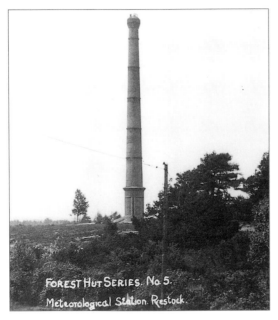

Meteorological station, Pyestock, 1915.
When Aldershot Camp was built in 1855 this
large incinerator with its 60 ft chimney was
built close to Norris Bridge to cope with the
vast amount of waste coming from the camps.
The army ceased to use the incinerator at the
turn of the century. Various instruments were
secured to the top of the chimney by the
Royal Aircraft Establishment from about 1910
until 1922 for the recording of wind speeds,
temperature, air purity and so on. By the time
that the RAE relinquished the site the building
was in danger of collapse, and it was
demolished in 1930.

Oakley's Stores, c. 1915. These premises on the corner of Upper Street and Fleet Road grew from the
original shop with house behind which opened in March 1885. Early in the 1890s the main shop with
clock tower was built on the corner and Albany Lodge at the end of the site in Fleet Road, to house the
growing Oakley family and some of the shop assistants. In earlier days water was provided by four wells,
three under the shop and house and the other by the stable block. In 1877, before James and Clara Oakley
came to Fleet, they had a shop and small cottage at Dogsmerfield. The business, Fleet's original
department store, closed in 1958/9.

Fleet News office, 1902, situated close to Barclays Bank. In about 1850 Mr Morgan started printing the *News* in a 25 ft by 15 ft brick workshop, using a printing press driven by a steam engine. The *2d* paper was delivered to the local newsagents at precisely 6 o'clock on Friday evenings. On the death of Mr Morgan local businesses and the gentry were left without a printer, and in the early 1900s many of these people became shareholders of the North Hants Printing Co., which was formed using Mr Morgan's premises and press. The company remained there until 1924 when new premises were built on land to the right of Stevens' garage. The business closed in 1967.

Fleet Hospital, 1904. The hospital was opened in 1897 after Lord Calthorpe had donated the ground, and a public subscription list quickly produced £444 for the building fund which Lord Calthorpe doubled. It was decided to built two four-bed and one private ward together with the usual offices; there would be two nursing staff, matron and nurse. There were no gas, electricity or sewage systems in Fleet at this time but a water supply was laid on. Daniel Poulter won the contract to build the hospital, for £638 10s 6d. Many improvements and extensions have been made over the years, mainly by public subscription.

Ruby Cottage, 1906. This Victorian house on the corner of Albert and Upper streets came on the market at about the time the Council was inaugurated in 1904, and they bought it for the offices and a yard. The yard at the back soon had a stable and shed for the three carts; later the new (motorised) fire engine was housed in the garage attached to the house. In the 1930s larger premises were required and it was at this time that Col. Horniblow, who had always been a councillor, offered his home, The Views in Reading Road, and the Council moved its offices. In the first few months of 1936 County Commercial Cars, which had occupied their factory at 127 Albert Street since 1929 (their offices were a couple of rooms nearby) bought the old Council Office site. County eventually sold the site in 1980 to Pilgrim Miller's, the business estate agents.

Council Offices, 1953. In 1936 Col. Horniblow, having already given his grounds (now The Views playing fields, which included what today is Campbells Close) to the people of Fleet, sold the house to the Council at an advantageous price. There was much more room on this site and a large fire station with garages for the refuse vehicles, etc. was built and an area fenced off for a storage yard. In the 1960s the adjacent Harlington House and the old Ebenezer Baptist Chapel were bought to increase the number of offices as the Council's area of jurisdiction was enlarged. After the formation of Hart District Council in 1974 it was obviously not economic sense to have half the staff in Fleet and the rest in Hartley Wintney, and in 1986 the present Civic Offices were built. The old buildings and the allotment site down the hill were sold to pay for the new building.

CHAPTER TWO

EDUCATION & RELIGION

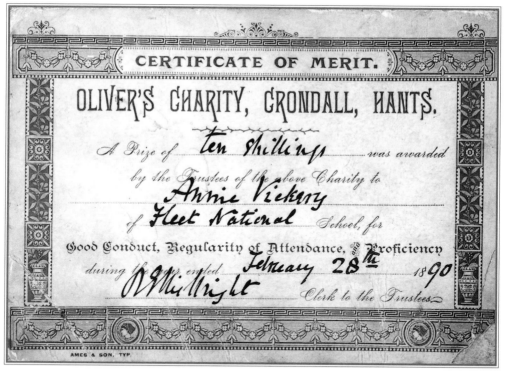

Certificate of Merit, 1890. Oliver's Charity was set up in Crondall in 1818 with a legacy to Mr Maxwell of Ewshot House from Mrs Oliver, his housekeeper, who wished her savings (£412 18s 5d) to be invested to benefit local children. The charity was regulated by an order of 1885 and initially a reward of 10s was given to those of good attendance at the local schools. The parishes of Fleet, Crookham and Crondall each received equal shares.

Dogmersfield School, 1927. The school was opened on the present site in Chatter Alley in 1911, and it can be presumed that there was a school, perhaps only a room in a house, there earlier. Miss Robinson (left) was headmistress and Miss Poulter was her assistant; there were over forty pupils between five and fourteen years old. Miss Robinson was teaching here in the 1920s and at least to the outbreak of the war, cycling to school each day from the Kings Road end of Albert Street where she lived with her sister, a teacher at Fleet School.

Crookham Infant School, 1917. The original school, which opened in 1843, was demolished in 1894 to be replaced by a larger building. The school was getting larger year by year: in 1853 there was one infant class, in 1911 two and by 1915 there were three. In 1911 Miss Chaston was promoted to Infant Headmistress and remained until 1925. Until the end of the war in 1945 the school holidays were adjusted by a week or two to allow the children to help in the harvesting of corn, hops and in earlier years tobacco.

Crookham Schools, 1958. This is the school in Gally Hill Road, built in 1911 to provide more classrooms. The original buildings were to the left of the new school and lay several yards back from the road. Education was provided here for children aged from five to fourteen years and like most schools built between the 1840s and the 1930s there were no grass play areas, just asphalt playgrounds. The toilets were located away from the school buildings, because of course when they were built there was no main drainage.

Fleet School, *c.* 1907. This no doubt was Empire Day, when the whole school celebrated together. The children stretch across Albert Street from the School House and on to the grass in front of the schoolroom. This building behind the fir tree is the only one left in Fleet where children from the C. of E. School were taught this century. The room has in recent times been used as offices and an antique shop. The timbered house was demolished before the war and the Rose Farm Dairy now uses the site as a garage for their milk floats.

Standard V, Fleet School, 1926. The class is at the front of the school facing Albert Street. Even in 1926 there were nearly fifty in the class. Fleet's first school was opened in 1860 close to the church in a cottage which still stands today; there were about thirty pupils. By 1863 the Church had taken over the school and ran it as a Church school. By 1885 the number of children to be educated was 120, so a new school was needed. Mr Brake, who had bought a large piece of Fleet at auction in 1878, sold the Church eighteen plots on the corner of Albert Street and Church Road at half price.

Fleet School, 1926. Another class of nearly fifty is arranged towards the lower end of the girls' playground. The building behind the group was the tool, coke and cycle sheds adjoining the toilets. In 1886 only the block in Albert Street was built, and it was not until 1910 that the Church Road block was required for the Infants' School.

War shrine, C. of E. School. This Roll of Honour was erected on the wall in the top class after the First World War flags were draped either side and fresh flowers were provided by the children. On the wall in Standard V, the top class for those who passed the 'scholarship', there was another Roll of Honour listing in gold the names of all the successful students. The names of the twelve or so who passed were added each year.

School prizegiving, 1931. Billy Parsons, one of Fleet School's governors, is holding the flagpole while he gives his speech at the annual event – when the top girls and boys receive books for their achievements. This ceremony took place at the back of the main school in the playground. In 1947, when Heatherside School was built, the senior pupils moved on from Albert Street, and when Courtmoor was opened in 1960 the juniors also left, leaving the whole school to the infants. Fleet Infants opened in January 1987 in Velmead Road, and the old Fleet School finally closed; it was later demolished to make way for the houses around Old School Close. Mr Parsons ran one of his family butcher's shops in Fleet Road, close to Church Road.

Miss Pickings' School, 1926. This school used the Methodist Sunday school room in Branksomewood Road from the end of the First World War until 1933. When Miss Pickings died two sisters named Ward opened a school nearby, in the same road, and within a year or two St Nicholas' School was opened. There were only eighteen houses in the road in 1936.

St Nicholas' School, 1946. This school was established in Branksomewood Road in 1937 by Miss Pritchard and Miss McKenzie; it prospered, and by 1996 occupied several large houses along the road. Its tennis courts went through to Victoria Road. The school has now moved to Redfields House in Redfields Lane, where it is under one roof and has large playing fields.

All Saints' Church, 1921. The foundation stone was laid in 1860 by Mr Lefroy, the squire of Crondall (which included Fleet), in memory of his wife Janet, but he died in 1861 before the church was finished. It was designed in the style of an Italian basilica, cost £3,323 and was consecrated in 1862, when the Rev. William Plummer was vicar. A beautiful tomb with marble recumbent figures of Mr and Mrs Lefroy rested by the choir stalls.

The interior of All Saints', 1902. This shows how the chancel was built with the Lefroys' tomb on the left. During 1934 the church was modified and lengthened at the back, and the opportunity was taken to move the tomb to the side of the extended north aisle to make more room for the choir. In 1974 the Meeting Room was added, mainly for use by the Sunday school.

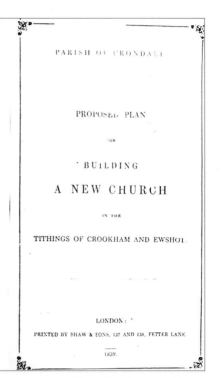

CROOKHAM AND EWSHOT CHURCH.

THE Parish of CRONDALL, in which it is proposed to build this Church, is wholly agricultural, consisting of about 10,000 acres, extending over an area of nearly six miles in length in a direct line, by from two and a half to three and upwards in breadth, and containing a population of 2,200 persons.

The Parish Church, which stands at one end of the parish, contains sittings for about 450 persons, of which not more than one third are free, while the tithings of EWSHOT and CROOKHAM, at the opposite end of the parish, contain a population of nearly 1,200 persons. Of these, 950 are at such a distance from the Parish Church that few of them frequent it at all; a considerable portion of them being more than two, and many more than three miles from it.

PARISH OF CRONDALL

PROPOSED PLAN
FOR
BUILDING
A NEW CHURCH
IN THE
TITHINGS OF CROOKHAM AND EWSHOT.

LONDON:
PRINTED BY SHAW & SONS, 137 AND 138, FETTER LANE.
1839.

Part of a booklet issued by the clergy at Crondall, setting out the need for a church at Crookham.

7

Lord CALTHORPE has kindly interested himself in the case, and has consented, with the following gentlemen, to act as a Committee to carry the above object into effect, by each of whom any subscriptions will be most thankfully received, viz.

The Rev T. A. WARREN, *Rural Dean, South Warnboro.'*
Rev. C. DYSON, *Dogmersfield.*
Rev. W. D. HARRISON, the Vicar,
Rev. E. J. WHITE, the Curate,
Rev. A. C. LEFROY
Major BIRCH . . . . } *Crondall.*
J. A. JOHNSTON, Esq. . . . .
and
C. E. LEFROY, Esq. . . . . .

THE FOLLOWING SUBSCRIPTIONS HAVE BEEN RECEIVED OR PROMISED

	£	s	d
The Right Rev. the Bishop of Winchester	50	0	0
The Right Hon. Lord Calthorpe	200	0	0
The Dean and Chapter of Winchester	100	0	0
Rev C. Dyson (from a fund at his disposal)	200	0	0
Major Birch	100	0	0
Mrs. Lefroy	100	0	0
C. E. Lefroy, Esq.	100	0	0
Rev. W. D. Harrison, Vicar (besides endowment) }	25	0	0
Mrs. Waldo	15	0	0
Sir J. Richardson	10	0	0
Rev. E. Hawkins	5	0	0
Rev. T. A. Warren	5	0	0
J. Quilter, Esq	5	5	0
W. Tillotson, Esq	1		0
Rev. T. A. Maberly	1		0
J. Dickenson, Esq.			0
C. Richardson, Esq			0

The committee, and subscriptions received or promised for the church. It was estimated that the church would have to seat 400 people.

Christ Church, 1920s. The church at Church Crookham was built and consecrated in 1841 by Bishop Sumner of Winchester. It also served Ewshot until 1872, when their own St Mary's Church was built. While the Rev. Gordon Wickham was vicar (1875–83) a large chancel was built; the addition included a side aisle for children's seats, which made room for more adults' seats in the transepts. The church was transferred to the newly created Diocese of Guildford in 1927.

Christ Church Mothers' Union, 1950. The Mothers' Union met in a member's sitting room in the early days, then the WI Hall by the Verne and later the Memorial Hall, until the meeting room was built in 1971. The Rev. John Langridge was the vicar in the 1950s, and on his right in this photograph is Mrs Wynne, a member for many years and a one-time leader. The banner was made locally in the early years of the century and a new central panel with Virgin and Child was made in the late 1940s.

SS Philip and James' Church, 1940. The daughter church was consecrated in 1900 to meet the needs of the growing population in the Kings Road/Pondtail area. The construction was simple and cheap, being corrugated-iron sheets on a timber frame with a wood lining; it was known to many as the iron church.

The altar, SS Philip and James' Church, just before the alterations of 1920. After the church had been standing for sixty years the timbers were rotting and beyond repair. When it was decided to build a new church, a site close to Pondtail was sought and eventually Fernhurst was chosen. In 1966 the new church with hall and car park adjacent were opened on the one site. The old church site, now P. and J. Court for elderly people, was sold after the organ and various fittings were taken up the road to the new church.

SS Philip and James' Church, 1943. The choirs of both churches were always strong and it was not until the 1950s that there were spaces available for girls. This was the choir in the days of the Rev. I.W. Moir with the choirmaster Mrs Humphries. At one time there were three generations of the Hoare family in the choir: long service was the norm in those days.

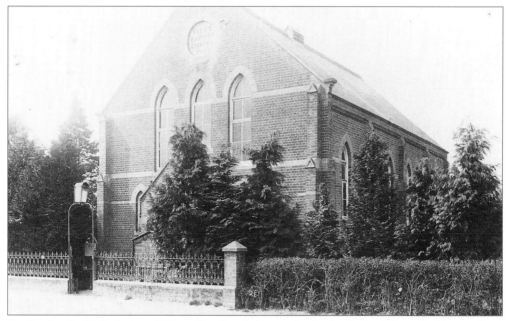

Baptist church, 1905. Built in 1893 in Fleet Road close to the Oatsheaf, this 200-seat building replaced the original Hope Chapel in Reading Road close to Hagley Road. By 1922 there was a Sunday school room behind the church, which was constructed of materials from the old Hope Chapel. This room was used as an extra classroom for Albert Street School during the war when Fleet had so many evacuees, and housed the top class. After a 1961 road widening scheme at the Oatsheaf corner the frontage was lost, so there were just a couple of steps out of the church on to the pavement. When the present church in Clarence Road was opened in 1965 the old site was sold for development.

Wesleyan Methodist church, 1910. This brick and stone church was erected on the corner of Branksomewood Road and Fleet Road in 1899 to replace a smaller 1887 wooden building on the site. A Sunday school room and kitchen with plenty of tables and several ovens and sinks were built behind the church. There were no domestic science facilities at the Albert Street School, therefore a crocodile of girls from the top two classes could be seen wending its way to Branksomewood Road every Monday morning to use the church facilities. The two Methodist churches united in 1963, with morning worship in this church and evensong in Reading Road. When the church was demolished in the late 1960s Woolworths moved in, and nearly forty years later they are still there.

Sunday school outing, 1911. Most children went to Sunday school and the summer treat for the Wesleyans was an outing to Elvetham or Dogmersfield Park, where teas were provided after games and races. The ride in a horse-drawn brake was a real treat. Later Frensham, Hindhead and Bognor were visited by charabanc. In 1938, 1939 and again for several years after the war a special train was laid on by Charlie Perrin to Bournemouth and Swanage.

'A New Primitive Methodist Chapel', 1883. The poster gives an invitation to the foundation stone-laying ceremony and tea, followed by an address in the Baptist chapel in the evening. A local publication dated 1874 mentions a Primitive Methodist church which had been built for £100, but nobody has seen another mention of this church or where it was built. This notice is for a 'new' church, perhaps more evidence that an old one existed.

Primitive Methodist church, 1921. As a result of the fund-raising events the church was consecrated in 1884 on the site of the present post office opposite Heatherside School. A Sunday school room was added in 1898 and the vestry in 1916. When the Primitive and Wesleyan wings of Methodism united the church in Fleet Road was sold, and it was decided to build a modern church by the side of the earlier Primitive church; this was opened in 1972. The new post office was then built where the old church had stood.

Crookham war memorial, 1923. After the First World War, when the servicemen returned home, there was a rush to build memorials in the towns and villages to commemorate those who had fallen. Crookham decided on a simple cross on a stone base. Subscriptions poured in, and the war memorial was erected and unveiled in 1921 – having been made by Mardles of Fleet, stonemasons. In the late 1940s the base was modified to show the fallen in the Second World War, and it still stands on the triangle formed by the junction of Gally Hill and Gables roads close to the church.

Fleet war memorial, 1921. The memorial was originally sited at the junction of Fleet and Minley roads backing on to the Station Hotel (now Links Hotel). The Earl of Selborne, the local Member of Parliament, unveiled the memorial in April 1921. Mardles were again the stonemasons and they added the names of the fallen in the Second World War. Owing to the increase in the volume of traffic passing along the road while the Remembrance service was being held the memorial was moved in the 1970s to the library precinct, and a further move was necessary when the Civic Offices were built in 1986.

CHAPTER THREE

RETAIL

Pondtail post office, 1912. This house was built just before the turn of the century and it was a sub-post office before 1910. It is one of the last corner shops in Fleet, and is situated opposite Wood Lane.

Byrnes newsagent, 1928. Byrnes opened their business in a wooden building in 1922 in what was then Green Lane. By 1932 the hut had been replaced by the present house and shop on the same site. The road was renamed Beacon Hill Road in 1936 and the family are still running the business over seventy years on.

T.H. Mellerish and Son, 1908. Almost opposite Award Road in Gally Hill Road there were three shops: Mellerish, Dr Frere's surgery (later a bootmaker) and a butcher's. Two were converted to houses by 1937 and Mr Mellerish closed in 1938. The residents of this area must have been less than pleased when they closed, as the nearest shop then would have been half a mile away.

Jessett's Stores, 1903. This shop was on the junction of Crondall and Pilcot roads. The Jessett family opened the business in 1843 and it closed in the 1960s. Delivery vehicles (horse and carts in the early days) took the various goods to outlying areas like Crondall, Winchfield, Fleet and Elvetham. For many years Jessett's was the only shop in the village and it catered for the needs of everyone with bread, grocery, greengrocery, clothing and haberdashery – and of course it was the post office.

A. Crumplin, 1940. In 1934 Alf Crumplin built a house and shop complete with hairdressing salon on the corner of Reading Road and Albert Street. Alf with his 'boy' (Fred Godden, who must have spent forty years with Alf) started the business in a single-storey building opposite in Reading Road in 1925. In the early 1960s Alf died and his wife continued to run the shop with Fred in the salon, and business boomed when a new assistant barber was brought in – a young lady (the first female barber in Fleet). The property was compulsorily purchased for a road-widening scheme, and Fred then cycled to give clients a short back and sides in their own sitting rooms for a few years. The road widening didn't take place but the Council built Woodman Court on the site, a block of flats for single people.

Church Crookham post office, on the corner of Aldershot Road and Sandy Lane, 1936. Mr Goddard altered his house in 1908 to include a shop and sub-post office in the front room. Mr Liming, a well-known name in Church Crookham, built the house and he left his trademark, a monkey puzzle tree – which stood in the garden until a few years ago. It was removed when the junction was improved. After the war the post office closed, and today it is sited in the Verne.

E. Field, 1927. Mr Field's first shop, which he built himself, had an unusual roof line and was next to the restaurant in Reading Road opposite Glen Road. The business of 'Musical and Cycle Store' opened in 1920 and transferred along the road to almost opposite Albert Street when W.C. Baker moved out in 1935. Mr Field's old shop became a general store and was demolished by Heanes in the 1970s.

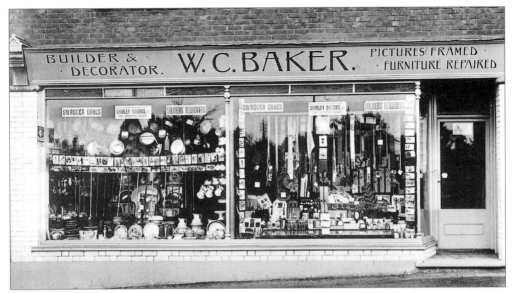

W.C. Baker, 1926. Mr Baker moved into Blenheim House in 1908 and opened a hardware shop there. In 1935 the family moved round to Fleet Road next to what is now Gurkha Square car park and built a new home and shop on part of Chernocke House grounds. Having to move out of Blenheim House before their new place was ready, they took a shop next to Lloyds Bank for a year. They occupied their new premises in 1936 and are still there today, the longest serving family business in Fleet. The shop today is run by the third and fourth generations of the Baker family.

E. Field, 1936. The cycle shop moved up the road to larger premises at Blenheim House vacated by Bakers in 1935; there was now a large showroom and more space to carry out repairs. The cycle shop remained here until 1988, by now managed by the third generation of the family, when a move was made to the end of the block of shops on the eastern corner of the Fleet and Reading roads.

F.J. Tayler, 1912. The jewellery and watch repair business spanned the period from 1908 to the 1970s on the eastern corner of Fleet and Reading roads. Between the wars F.J. retired and his son A.G. carried on the business; small boys (and bigger ones) would stand for ages at the side window and watch Mr Tayler in his workshop with his magnifying glass fixed to his eye. Originally the property stretched down to Albert Street, but in 1934 the piece on that corner was sold to Mr Crumplin for his shop, and a plot next door was sold for a bungalow.

Cane's Stores, 1930. Cane's opened in the late nineteenth century on the northern corner of Fleet and Reading roads. The salesmen would visit the homes of the gentry each morning to solicit orders for that day's delivery; delivery boys on cycles for small orders or the horse-drawn cart for bigger ones would ensure they arrived promptly. By 1930 motor vans were in use for an even faster service. The premises were demolished in the mid-1960s and the parade of shops on the corner today occupy the site of the Baptist church and Cane's.

Osmond's, 1913. In about 1906 Mr Osmond lived in a four-bedroomed house next to Mr Tayler's on the corner of Fleet and Reading roads. He foresaw that Fleet was going to grow fast, and he soon built a large single-storey shop across the front of his house. Pneumatic tyres had just been introduced and bicycles were lighter because of new technology, and sales were growing as everybody wanted a machine. The roads were not metalled and the flints caused many punctures. Mr Osmond employed a man to mend a tube while you waited. He later sold prams, high chairs and cots, and remained in business until the mid-1950s.

E. Wright, 1911. Mr Wright was related to the operator of the mill in Minley Road and he started selling animal feed from the mill to local smallholdings and stables in the district. Most houses kept chickens and many had pigs; all these householders would be customers of the corn merchant. Mr Wright, whose shop was almost opposite today's entrance road to Gurkha Square car park, had left the shop by 1920.

J. Parrott, 1912. This newsagent and tobacconist was directly opposite the entrance road to Gurkha Square car park and was trading from 1908 to 1992. Mr and Mrs Parrott owned the business from 1910 but the family sold it in the 1950s. Various people owned the paper shop until Forbuoys finally closed it.

Nelson and Goodrick, 1908. Originally this business occupied two shops, with Richardson's in between. The lower shop sold furniture while the other was a draper's; but eventually the lease on the lower shop was not renewed. The remaining shop was altered so that there were windows either side of the central walkway; the front door and shop were several yards off the pavement. The firm remained in business until the 1950s; it was a first-class department store. Shelaugh Fashions took over for several years until the area was redeveloped early in the 1960s, and a modern block with ground floor shops and two floors of offices was built opposite the Gurkha Square car park.

Richardsons, 1912. Mr and Mrs Richardson were ironmongers also selling kitchenware and garden tools, and their shop opened in 1906 next to Nelson and Goodrick, opposite what is now Gurkha Square car park. Mrs Richardson was widowed after a few years but carried on the business until 1937 when she retired.

Chernocke House, 1953. Built in the 1880s, this became the surgery and home of Fleet's first doctor, Dr Gilbert Wickham. In 1910 Dr Slade was in residence and in the 1930s Dr Greenish came here for several years. By 1939 the building was used as the Fleet Bridge Club and a couple of flats. In the 1950s the library moved from its first home, two shops down the Fleet Road. When the present library was built in 1975 Chernocke House was demolished, and Gurkha Square car park was created.

P.R. Harden and Sons, 1925. As development continued along Fleet Road, Percy Harden built this shop in 1896 with living accommodation over and a slaughterhouse at the back. He was later joined in the business by his sons Percy and Tom. When the sons took over Tom soon left the business, opening a butcher's shop in Reading Road – next door but one to Tower House on the Fleet Road corner. Eventually Percy junior's son, another Percy, went into partnership with his father, and their business flourished (as did Tom's) until the area was sold for redevelopment in the early 1960s. The large office block opposite Gurkha Square car park replaced Harden's.

Rutter's, 1907. These premises on the corner of Fleet and Victoria roads were built early in the 1890s by Mr Rutter, who saw the need for a high-class butcher in the centre of the village. The premises next door were built at about the same time but as houses; they were not converted to shops until the 1920s. The two horse chestnut trees on the pavement were planted by Mr Rutter to shade his shop over a hundred years ago.

A.L. Mill, 1932. This single-storey shop was attached to a Victorian house, Carn Brea, in Upper Street, between Albert Street and Clarence Road. The shop with workroom behind was built by Mr Mill using building blocks he made himself. The business thrived until after the war when Mr Mill retired to Hayling Island. He was a keen bandsman and belonged to the Fleet Silver Band, even lending his workroom for band practice for several years. The site is now a bungalow and car park.

Oakley's and clock tower, 1920s. The property still stands today in the main road on the junction with Upper Street, having been mainly built in the 1890s. The earliest part was an existing shop which James and Clara Oakley moved to in 1885; they then built Albany Lodge adjoining the shop. Later additions gave them the premises which today are occupied by a public house. After the Oakleys retired in 1959 the premises were variously a freezer centre, carpet and furniture stores. The striking of the clock could be heard over much of Fleet in the early days but today's chimes can be heard only a few yards away. Princess Beatrice was a customer at the turn of the century; therefore the Royal Warrant was conspicuously displayed.

Capital and Counties Bank, 1920. Opened in 1889, this was a very imposing building, with its red granite porch pillars and its stone façade. It was surrounded by trees. Within ten years Lloyds Bank had bought the premises, and in 1970 the building had a facelift – with the façade and porch being removed. The granite pillars were taken to Goddard's builder's yard for future use and were never seen again. In 1995 the Trustee Savings Bank and Lloyds merged, and early in 1998 another facelift proclaimed 'Lloyds TSB', the first joint bank in the area.

W.J. Crick, 1903. About 100 yards from the Church Road junction in Fleet Road, this shop was on the left of the old Waitrose store and was built with living accommodation above in the late 1880s. It was the first shop in Fleet to sell national newspapers; Mr Crick also had a fine stock of picture postcards of the district (this is one of his cards), stationery and tobacco. The shop changed owners several times but always held the same range of goods, but in the early 1990s the main post office closed and Forbuoys then ran the sub-post office in their shop. After a couple of years they moved along the road to larger premises.

Fleet post office, 1907. Pictured just a year after opening, this fine building is still serving the public. When the post office was closed in May 1990 the premises reopened as a building society. The first post office opened in Fleet in 1901 close to the Oatsheaf, and moved to a new shop three doors west of the purpose-built office for a couple of years.

Post office staff, 1920s. The large gas lamp to illuminate the entrance can be clearly seen. From 1906 the sorting of mail was carried out in the office at the back of the building, with the postmaster living on the first floor. As the volume of mail and the staff required increased extra accommodation was built, and the first floor was made into offices. In 1988 the sorting office was moved to the trading estate by the station, and now staff work through the night sorting incoming mail ready for the postmen to deliver.

Peter Pan, 1948. This business occupied the shop which stood 40 yards west of Church Road next to the supermarket. When Frank Bell came out of the services in 1945 he opened a sports shop, but in 1950 he moved up and across Fleet Road to a shop vacated by Mr Pace, and gradually drapery took over from sports goods. The Hart Centre north entrance stands where Peter Pan once stood. Mr Bell's original shop was demolished some years ago and was replaced by a block of shops and offices around Church Road corner.

Williams and Wright, 1968. Mr George Wright opened this shop on the Church Road and Fleet Road corner before the turn of the century, selling corn feed and flour which came from his family's Fleet Mill. He opened another shop nearer the Oatsheaf and both soon had coal pens, as this fuel had replaced peat. Herbert Williams came into the business and they concentrated on the Church Road corner site selling coal at 1s 4d a cwt (112 lb): at the time of writing 1 cwt costs £7.40. Supplies came initially by canal, being offloaded at Reading Road and the coal wharf at Crookham; the railway took over in 1900, with 10 ton trucks being delivered to the station sidings.

Rose Farm Dairy, 1906. Mark Kimber owned Rose Farm in Reading Road behind the Prince of Wales, and in 1862 began delivering milk locally. Business boomed and he built a shop and dairy in Fleet Road 100 yards past Church Road; the dairy entrance for the horse-drawn milk floats was in Church Road. By 1920 Mr Cubby together with Mr Adams from Broomhurst Farm took over the dairy, but after the war Mr Adams had died and Mr Watts from Bramshottt Farm was supplying the milk. Some years later he took over the dairy and 130 years on it is still Rose Farm Dairy. More space was required in the 1950s, and they expanded back to Albert Street. Today their electric floats are garaged in the extension.

Mid-Southern Gas and Electric Co., 1954. Built in the 1930s, the large showroom was always full of gas fires, lamps, ovens and electrical appliances. Before nationalisation in 1947 both gas and electricity were controlled by one company, with their store and workshop at the back of the showroom. During the war the appliances on display would occasionally be moved to a corner to enable a large display area to be available for the Warship or War Weapons Weeks exhibitions. The premises were vacated by the Electricity Board in 1947 but the Gas Board stayed for several years until the shops were built on the old cinema site. The electricity showrooms were almost opposite the clock tower. The foreground on the left is now Birch Parade.

Saunders' Nurseries, 1945. These nurseries fronted on to Fleet Road where an office block now stands, almost opposite Birch Avenue. The property went through to Albert Street where the frontage was almost twice as long. There were not only glasshouses but also nursery gardens. Mr T. Ayres founded the nursery in the first few years of this century and in 1923 Mr Saunders took over; the nursery stayed in his family until the late 1960s when the site was redeveloped.

H. Bracknell, 1900. Early in the 1880s Mr Bracknell built a shop opposite Birch Avenue, and was soon able to offer timber, ironmongery, carpentry and building supplies. He had a sawmill which was always busy. Power for the site was provided by three large steam engines and generators; about twenty staff were employed. In about 1904 Mr Bracknell moved to larger premises in Farnborough and Mr Brothers bought the Fleet Road shop. His ironmongery and decorating business kept several staff busy, and his son was so interested in radio and electrical goods, which were becoming more popular and less expensive, that he built an extension on the side that included a studio for television. In 1939 there were about a dozen chairs provided, and here it was that many Fleet people had their first experience of television – including Test cricket!

Avondale post office, 1920. Built in 1908 as a single-storey shop and house, Mr Chorley was the postmaster; the shop was 'open for business daily from 8 a.m. to 8 p.m.' The premises sold tobacco, confectionery and stationery, including local view cards published by Mr Chorley. A second storey was added in the 1920s, and the premises were known as the Tuck Shop until rebuilt as a specialist tyre and wheel outlet in the early 1990s. The sub-post office transferred to a shop in the middle of the Avondale Parade in 1935, and stayed there until the post office was closed in the 1980s.

T.J. Norman, 1916. Mr Willis opened the tea rooms in 1904 but at the onset of the First World War Mr Norman had taken over; he remained in business until the 1950s. From the 1930s there was a covered area at the side of the shop where you could leave your cycle for 6d when you went on the train; there were no facilities at the station for cycles. The café did a good trade from the men working on the trucks in the railway sidings. There were half a dozen coal merchants and the camp generated a lot of business.

Donoghue's Stores, 1925. This property, on the corner of Pinewood Hill and Kings Road, was built in 1905 and was a true corner shop, with a wide range of products crammed into a tiny space. After Mrs Donoghue died in 1936 the shop closed, but reopened as a café during the war; it was later a ladies' and then gents' hairdresser. The family sold the property in 1972.

Vincent's, 1909. Mr Harold Vincent built the shop on the corner of Clarence and Kings roads in 1906, together with living accommodation and stables. He came from Chertsey and established himself as a high-class butcher, in the early days selling 'no frozen meat'. He also bought an acre of land at Pondtail where he raised chickens and produced eggs. This picture, which shows Harold with his two older children, Son and Ella, shows the power of advertising: even the telegraph pole is utilised! This type of display always attracted customers before Christmas – but what would the health officials say today? Two younger sons, Leslie and Derek, took over from their father and the business remained a thriving concern until it closed in 1982.

CHAPTER FOUR

LEISURE

Skating on Fleet Pond, c. 1905. Most years up to the 1950s the pond froze over for several weeks each winter, and hundreds of people could be seen playing ice hockey or curling or just skating. Until 1929 special trains ran from London to Fleet several times a week when skating was possible. Bonfires were lit on the islands and large parties were held most evenings.

Oddfellows' Fête, c. 1920. Fêtes were always large events, usually for the members of the local Friendly Societies and often held in the meadow close to Woodlands by Birch Avenue. The Buffaloes, Hampshire Friendly Society, Rechabites and Oddfellows would join together, and one of the Fleet bands would lead the procession through the town. Pride of place in the procession would go to the beautiful large banners of each organisation. All societies would look after their members and their families in the event of sickness, death or unemployment – and all for a couple of pence a week.

Fishing at Malthouse Bridge, 1908. The canal, being quite weed-free after just a hundred years' use by the thousands of laden barges which had plied along its length, was ideal for fishing. Various reaches were called 'deeps', and here shoals of various species would congregate. Fishing is still very popular along the length of the canal, and small numbered discs are in evidence as peg markers for fishing matches.

Boating on the canal, 1905. Boathouses sprang up close to bridges near areas of population, with Ash Vale, Wharf, Reading Road, Chequers, Barley Mow and Colt Hill bridges being the largest nearby. Often owners of the Bridge Stores would have a small number of boats in the boathouse on the other side of Reading Road Bridge.

Boathouse, Reading Road Wharf, 1935. Various people held the licence to hire boats here over the last century but the most successful were Mr Cox and his son: they had the lease during the Second World War when hundreds of troops would hire punts, canoes and rowing boats of various types to take their girlfriends to a quiet spot.

Canal Carnival, 1926. The landlord of the Fox and Hounds close to the cemetery could always see the potential of extra trade if he organised a regatta or decorated boat festival on the canal behind the premises. This entrant shows how elaborate the entries were. Even today a couple of events a year are held at the Fox and Hounds.

Forest Hut Café, 1928. This wooden café was open at weekends during the summer, and did a good trade with rowers from Wharf and Reading Road bridges. The outbreak of war in 1939 spelled the end of this business, as the house and café were left empty and it was soon used for hand grenade practice. After the war Farnborough Airfield was fenced off, and the site of part of this property is now inside the fence.

Crookham Mummers, 1912. Boxing Day is the only day the Mummers perform, and they now give three performances – at the Chequers, the Black Horse and The Crescent. They have enacted the same play for more than 100 years, and its origins are obscure. The players, who include Bold Roamer, King George, Turkish Knight, Father Christmas and Trim Tram, wear coats and hats decorated with strips of paper.

Fleet Fanciers' Show card, 1910. Fleet Fanciers' Society held its annual show in the Pinewood Hall. The society was founded in 1904 and soon increased its interest from poultry to include cats, dogs, caged birds and rabbits.

Fleet Brownies, 1916. In their early days the Brownies met in benefactors' gardens in the summer, or when sufficient cash had been raised would move to a small hall. Mrs Slingo was their leader. Eighty years on, and the numbers of Guides, Brownies and Rainbows can be counted in their hundreds in Fleet and Crookham.

Fleet Boy Scouts, 1936. A group photograph with the District Trophy (with a wolf's head on top of the pole), which was won by the Cubs, and the President's Trophy Flag. The 22nd Odiham Group leaders were Mrs Sergeaunt (seated) and Maurice Hill. Standing are John Mill, Maurice Hill, Ray Blount and Tony Mearing. Seated are Stan Butt and Joe Standen with cubs Don Ancell, Geoff Barton, Maurice Bone and Jimmy Dove.

Summer Scout camp, Odiham, 1912. This shows the fine catering arrangements. These camps were always popular, as for most boys it was the only time that they were away from home.

Sir Seymour Hicks and Miss Ellaline Terriss, 1930s. In the early 1930s Seymour and his wife came to Fleet and bought The Courtyard in Elvetham Road. This had been the laundry of Stockton House and had remained empty after the house was sold. Seymour was knighted in 1935. During the war they entertained the troops, and remained in South Africa until 1946. They were both born in 1871. Ellaline, whose father was a sheep farmer, was born in the Falklands, but the family moved back to England where her father became a respected actor. At the age of fifteen she danced in *Sinbad the Sailor* with Vesta Tilley. She met Seymour, and after only eighteen days he proposed; they were married a few weeks later in 1889. Sir Seymour died in 1949 and his wife (aged 100) in 1971. They are buried in Fleet Cemetery with a white marble stone over the double grave.

Aldershot Tattoo, 1936. 'First Prince of Wales' was one of the tableaux enacted at this annual event. The tattoo started in the 1890s as a military fête and bazaar for Queen Victoria at the Royal Pavilion. In 1922 the show became the Searchlight Tattoo on Cove Common, and the next year it moved to the purpose-built Rushmoor Arena with two large grandstands seating 60,000 people; it ran for ten days with royalty present each night. The attendance exceeded half a million in 1939, but the war meant the end of the tattoos. The Aldershot Show was (and still is) held at the Arena, and in the summer thousands of OCTU and Territorials would spend their camp here.

Fleet station, 1930. Up to ten excursion trains a night would arrive at Fleet station between 7 p.m. and 9.30 p.m. on Wednesday, Friday and Saturday evenings of both weeks of the tattoo from all parts of the country: the Great Western from Wales, the LMS from Manchester and Liverpool, the LNER from York and Newcastle and the Southern from Weymouth, Exeter and so on. These trains would be met by forty or so Traction Co. buses, which quickly did the round trip to Rushmoor to keep the queue short. Hundreds of cars and charabancs would come over the station bridge, while hundreds of local people gathered at the station and along Kings Road to watch the traffic: the most Kings Road normally saw was twenty cars, one lorry and a tank each day. The tattoo brought the area noisy excitement every year – and this was duplicated in Farnborough and Aldershot.

Fleet Lido, 1949. In the early 1930s a house was built on the right of the Small Pond next to the Mission Room in Cove Road. Within a few years a public outdoor swimming pool was added behind it. Local children swam in the pond and canal with no apparent ill effects before the pool was open. Boys and girls in their last two years at Crookham and Fleet schools walked to the pool weekly between Easter and summer if it was warm enough. From 1947 (when the senior pupils had moved to Heatherside) there were very occasional lessons at the pool. Houses stand on the whole site today.

Peer Gynt, early 1930s. This performance of the once-popular operetta was given by the Crookham Women's Institute. The WI Hall in those days was in Aldershot Road where today the Verne has been built. In the latter part of the war a stick of bombs just missed the camp, landing in Sandy Lane, Aldershot Road and the last one very close to the WI Hall. The Women's Institute is still very active in Crookham, with both Church Crookham and the village having groups.

Snow White and the Seven Dwarfs, Fleet Carnival, 1938. This was the Hesters' entry, with daughter and son together with their friends. Bert Hester had a garage in Upper Street (his daughter is still a director today) and he was always a great supporter of carnivals. Before the war the carnival was held to aid the hospital, which was kept open by voluntary subscriptions. The procession started at the station and proceeded to the Oatsheaf, then down Reading Road and on to the field at Courtmoor House. Some dwellings about 30 yards back but facing Reading Road had been built at this time, but behind these there were no houses. The 1939 event was the last before the war and we had to wait until the early 1950s for the next.

Vincent's barrel organ, 1936. This was an entry in the Hospital Carnival. Each year these floats raised hundreds of pounds. Strong support for the procession was assured, as the traders were getting good publicity while supporting the cause.

Legion of Frontiersmen, 1938. The Legion was a local organisation led by Fred Liming of Reading Road. Members wore blue tunics with chainmail on the shoulders and Canadian Mountie-style hats; their horses were well trained and well turned out. The various fêtes were enhanced by the procession along Fleet Road with the banners of the Friendly Societies, and larger crowds would be drawn when the Frontiersmen also paraded. The events took place on the field near Birch Avenue, The Views or The Firs (now the police station), and the horsemen would on some occasions put on a display including tent pegging and jumping.

Fleet Youth Club, 1946. This photograph was taken at the opening of Fleet Youth Club in Kings Road Broadway by the Rt Hon. Oliver Lyttleton MP for Aldershot (which included Fleet), accompanied by Lady Crookshank. The leader of the club was Mr E.T.J. Tapp of Kings Road. The club was open most evenings, with rooms catering for snooker, table tennis, darts and drama.

Warship Week procession, 1942. The children joined the main procession at the school in Albert Street and went along Fleet Road to the Oatsheaf and down to the cricket ground. During the war various 'weeks' were organised: in 1940 the Spitfire Fund; in 1941 War Weapons and in this year Warship Week. The idea was to encourage everybody to buy Savings Certificates (15s each), thereby providing money for weapons, etc. Fleet and Crookham saved enough money to buy a corvette named *Itchen*. There was a ceremony daily during the week when the 'indicator' would be adjusted to show the total collected.

Model corvette, 1942. Built around a lorry, this boat was parked at strategic sites during Warship Week, and of course it headed the procession around the streets on the Saturday. Here the vehicle is parked in front of Dr Greenish's house, opposite today's police station.

Victory celebration tea, 1945. In spite of the strict rationing which was still in force, plenty of sandwiches and cakes were made for these parties. This one was outside Marlborough Villas in Clarence Road, a few yards from Church Road. Traffic was not a problem as very few people were running their cars: petrol rationing had not been relaxed yet.

Victory celebration tea, 1945. This party for local children was held in the Salvation Army Hall in Albert Street at the junction of Reading Road. Very few children would be absent and very few parents would not help with these parties; after five years of war everybody worked together.

Fleet Carnival Band, 1958. Alex Fitzpatrick is the local lad leading the band. He had a way of enlisting his friends to dress up and entertain the public: thus began several years of the Carnival Band. He persuaded any of his friends who could play a musical instrument (or who were willing to learn) to join, and borrowed instruments from the now defunct Fleet Brass Band. Several members were trained during their time in the services and on the day they presented a balanced band, but it was also the topical uniforms that enthralled the crowds.

Fleet Carnival Band, 1964. This year they saluted Tony Hancock with the East Cheam Colonials; previously we had seen in 1958 (above) St Trinian's All Girl Band (after the film) and in 1959 the 13th Suez Canal Lancers (after the Suez invasion). Late in 1966 the Trustees sold the remaining instruments belonging to the old Fleet Brass Band, and that killed off the Carnival Band.

CHAPTER FIVE

UNIFORMS

Fleet Section Territorial Army, 1909. This group of local men met at the Gymnasium in Albert Street (now Victoria Court) twice a week for drill. Sergeant Creeper of Clarence Road was in charge. The Territorial Army was formed in 1908, and this section was previously part of E Company of the 4th Battalion Hampshire Regiment. They are shown here at camp on Salisbury Plain.

Tweseldown Racecourse, 1903. This Army steeplechase course is close to the North Horns, and various hunts hold point-to-point meetings here in the spring, while other facilities make it suitable for three-day events. When Aldershot Camp was built in 1885–6 the Queens Parade Ground at North Camp was soon used as a racecourse (flat), and Tweseldown was laid out with its jumps ready for the first event in 1867 – mainly for the cavalry. Parts of the course were used for the equestrian events in the 1948 Olympic Games.

Officers' Quarters, Ewshot Camp, 1907. The entrance to Leipzig Barracks was just past the North Horns and stretched across towards Ewshot Lane; it was the permanent home of the Royal Field Artillery. Attached to the barracks were the Quetta and Punjab married quarters. The whole site was cleared in the 1970s, and Quetta Park married quarters were rebuilt close to Ewshot Lane.

Royal Field Artillery, 1914. No doubt from Ewshot Camp, they are passing down Crookham Street to Pilcot Road. This Brigade could be on its way to Salisbury Plain for summer manoeuvres, a trip that could take several days.

Tweseldown Camp. The camp at Crookham crossroads gave a great deal of work during construction to local tradesmen and craftsmen; within a year the camp was occupied. Haig Lines, as it was later called, was the home for Hungarians who fled to Britain after the uprising in 1956. They were later dispersed to homes all over the country. Later, troops about to do their spell of duty in Northern Ireland would train in the camp for 'house search' training assisted by the Gurkhas from down the road at Queen Elizabeth Barracks.

Haig Lines, 1914. Various units used the camp during the war. The areas between the 'Lines' was grassed over, with flower beds bordered by the regulation whitewashed stones. Soldiers who offended and were 'confined to barracks' would have to spend time repainting the stones. The camp was demolished in the 1980s and was replaced by a housing estate.

Crookham crossroads, 1923. Haig Lines became the Depot of the Royal Army Medical Corps in 1915; it remained here until 1932 when they moved to Keogh Barracks, Mychett – staying there until the outbreak of the war in 1939.

Inside a barrack room, 1915. This would be the scene at 7.45 every morning in all the huts: everything spotlessly clean, folded precisely and laid out exactly in its place. Broom handles would be scraped with a razor to keep them clean.

Miss Daniels Soldiers' Home, 1940. Marwell Lodge in Aldershot Road, near the Foresters, was rented as a Miss Daniels Home during the Second World War. Mrs Daniels was an officer's widow who in 1862 (just six years after Aldershot Camp was built) decided that soldiers should have somewhere to relax other than in a public house; so she raised funds and rented houses in areas with camps. During the last war her successors were still carrying on her work. All the homes were equipped with lecture, writing and games rooms just for soldiers.

Queen Elizabeth Barracks, 1950. This camp was built in 1938 for Militia Training (readiness for war) in Sandy Lane close to the Wyvern, with the RASC providing the staff. By 1940 the RAMC had moved back because their Mychett Barracks were now too small to train thousands of medics, and they stayed here until 1964 when they moved back to Keogh. In 1971 the Gurkhas came to Queen Elizabeth Barracks, and all of their regiments have been in residence since. They are due to move to Sheerness in 2000, when the last wooden-hutted camp in the country will be demolished.

Queen Elizabeth's visit, 1948. On 23 June 1948 Queen Elizabeth (now the Queen Mother) visited the RAMC at their Depot and Training Centre at Boyce Barracks, on the occasion of the Corps Golden Jubilee. The camp was named after a former GOC of the RASC, who were the first unit to use the camp. The camp became Queen Elizabeth Barracks on this day in honour of their Colonel-in-Chief. The Queen lunched with the officers at their Redfield House mess. In the afternoon she toured the Barracks, and as can be seen met the wives of some of the staff.

R. A. Horses Taking Swimming Lessons.

Horses swimming, 1906. Horses are natural swimmers but cavalry horses had to be trained to swim in pairs, with their riders and to swim from A to B; their natural tendency is to get out of the water.

Cavalry Swimming Horses, Aldershot

Cavalry Horse Pond, 1910. The 2½-acre pond was at Long Bottom close to Bourley, and here you can see the lines to which the horses were attached as they swam across. Many horses were lost over the years as thousands passed through this training, and in 1912 two soldiers who had drowned here were commemorated in St George's Garrison Church by a plaque on the wall. This area was the training ground for all of Aldershot's cavalry horses.

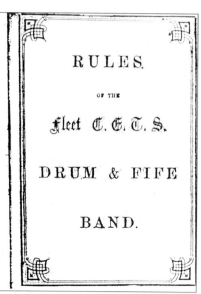

RULES

1.—That this Band shall be called "THE FLEET CHURCH OF ENGLAND TEMPERANCE SOCIETY DRUM-AND-FIFE BAND."

2.—That each Member shall be a total abstainer, and pay a weekly subscription of 2d. to the Band Fund.

3.—That the Bandmaster shall choose the music to be played.

4.—That every Member shall attend each practise for three months after joining the Band, unless exempted by the Bandmaster as efficient; after this every Member to attend one practise weekly (unless positively prevented) or pay a fine of 2d.

5.—That no Member will be permitted to bring any friend to the practise, except to introduce him as a Member, or by permission of the Bandmaster.

6.—That anyone wishing to join the Band after April, 1886, shall pay an entrance fee of 6d., which shall include that week's contribution; and all fines and subscriptions shall go to the Band Fund.

7.—That anything bought out of the fund shall belong to the Band, and any Member leaving the Band shall return all property belonging to the Band in good condition, or pay the value thereof.

8.—That any Member leaving the Band shall forfeit all claim or share in any articles or funds of the Band.

9.—That no Member shall write his name or make any mark in his music book, without the consent of the Bandmaster; play his instrument out of turn on practise night; or play his instrument to or from the place of practise.

10.—That any Member being four weeks in arrears with his subscriptions shall receive notice to that effect, and if he shall not pay in one week shall be fined 2d., and not be allowed to practise till his fine and subscription is paid.

11.—That no smoking be allowed in the band-room, or when playing on the march. Members using obscene or indecent language will be fined 3d.

Approved by the Commitee.

T. HORNIBLOW
H. PARNELL } *Hon. Secs.*

April 1st, 1887.

RULES

OF THE

Fleet C. E. T. S.

DRUM & FIFE

BAND.

Drum and Fife Band, 1887. The Church of England Temperance Society formed this band in 1886. It was founded by Colonel Horniblow, and Mr Parnell was the bandmaster. The rules are very strict but the threat of being fined must have been a deterrent. The band was always invited to accompany the banners of the Friendly Societies on fête days.

Fleet Wesleyan Band, 1913. The band in their smart blue uniforms always paraded with the banners of the Friendly Societies on fête days. The band was based at the Wesleyan Methodist Church Hall and was formed in the early years of the century; in later years it became Fleet Brass Band.

Fleet's first fire appliance, 1905. After a disastrous fire at Richard Pool's (in the background), when several horses were killed in their stables, and a couple of serious house fires, business people demanded a fire service and in 1900 Fleet Volunteer Fire Brigade was formed. They had no pumps but Mr Pool provided a horse, cart and stable; the hoses were connected direct to the mains. Hoses and standpipe were carried in the cart and the men in their uniforms and helmets cycled to the fire. It is related that one particular horse on hearing the alarm bells would get excited and kick his stable until the crew arrived; the noise woke residents in Albert Street.

Fire escape ladder and crew, 1904. Crookham had their own Brigade under Fleet Council, with two handcarts to carry the 470 yards of hose, standpipe and the fire escape ladder. By 1910 there were eight firemen, including the foreman: unlike Fleet they had to run to the fires. The fire station was opposite the Wyvern and the siren was in Gally Hill Road.

Firemen and cart, 1904. This was the crew taken over by the Council, and some of the equipment carried in their cart is on display. By 1920 they had a Model T Ford which carried the ladder, hoses and crew; this was kept in the garage of the Council Offices adjacent to Upper Street.

Fire engine and crew, 1934. This year a Dennis engine with a built-in pump to increase the water pressure was purchased. It had increased speed and better road-holding. The engine was kept in the garage in Albert Street until 1936, when the Council moved to The Views and a new fire station was built at the end of the tree-lined drive which is now by the side of Gurkha Square car park.

Fire at Burt's and Royal Dairy, 1908. G.E. Burt's newsagent and tobacconist's shop was gutted by a fire in 1908 and the Royal Dairy next door was badly damaged. When the newsagent's shop was rebuilt it was taken over by Mr and Mrs Parrott; the Royal Dairy reopened and only closed at the outbreak of war. The shops were opposite the entrance road to Gurkha Square car park.

Fire at Parnell's stables, 1930. The wooden stables and outbuildings behind the shops opposite Gurkha Square car park were destroyed by a disastrous fire; much stock was lost when the paraffin tank split. The fire brigade prevented the flames spreading to the shops and Mr Parnell rebuilt the outbuildings in brick.

Decontamination squad, 1943. Recruitment for Civil Defence began in 1937–8 owing to the threat of war. Lt-Col. A.E.S. Fennell was appointed Controller of Civil Defence and soon the various sections were built up, some at Pool's near the station (now the business park) and others in the yard by The Views. The purpose of decontamination was to identify the type of gas being used in an air raid and to employ the correct chemical to neutralise its effect.

Home Guard, 1944. No. 5 HQ Platoon, C Coy, 25th Hampshire Battalion Home Guard were based at County Commercial Cars in Albert Street, where at least seventeen members worked. The platoon learnt many of the disciplines taught to regular soldiers, and as well as night and weekend exercises many nights were spent guarding the gasholder at Pondtail Bridge and the length of railway. Lt-Col. Fennell, who was a well-known Fleet figure, is pictured second from left in the front.

CHAPTER SIX

TRANSPORT

White's steam engine, 1907. Grove Farm in Crookham Street used this steam engine for various tasks for many years. Its principal uses were thrashing the corn (separating the grain from the straw), removing dead trees and sawing logs. The belt driving the thrasher was driven by the large flywheel above the back wheel. The family took over the farm in the 1890s and they are still in residence today.

Steam engine and pantechnicon, 1900. Richard Pool owned the site between Fleet Road and Albert Street. A multi-storey depository and later two facing covered parking bays were built for the vehicles. Three Foden steam engines were parked at night around the corner at 127 Albert Street, a corrugated building belonging to a relative, Mr Pool of Ewshot. Half a ton of coal was always carried to 'feed' the engines, and on overnight trips the crew slept in the van. These iron horses were kept on the road until the 1920s, when parliament put a heavy road tax on them.

Horse vans, 1910. Local deliveries and removals were made by Richard Pool with these teams of vans, and the number to be seen indicates that this was a large business. By 1920 motor furniture vans were in use, with the fleet size growing to six vans and four or five tippers — mainly carrying coal and coke from the station sidings to the camps.

Motor pantechnicon, 1946. Immediately after the war this Jensen was built in the 'new' material, aluminium. The war had brought about so many developments in materials, uses and production methods that almost everything had changed. This vehicle was 30 ft long, very high and extremely light; therefore with an engine twice the horse-power of its pre-war predecessor it could carry a much larger load. In the late 1950s Richard Pool's was sold to Cantays of Basingstoke, and the site was sold.

Steam lorry, 1912. Mr Stevens ran his business from his home in Connaught Road, where Hartsleaf Close has since been built. He had a Foden steam lorry for many years and later used a petrol-engined lorry on local haulage work.

Recovery lorry with car, 1923. Ian Bradley built a garage in Fleet Road almost opposite Stockton Avenue in 1920; the showroom and office fronted the main road and access to the garage and paint shop (little more than a large garage) was from Albert Street. The recovery lorry was a Scammell with the first drop-frame trailer in Fleet. Here they had just recovered a 1921 Lanchester. The paint shop on the left of the site in Albert Street was a do it yourself business from the 1950s to the 1980s. Ian Bradley went into partnership with Mr Mathews in 1928 and they closed the business at the outbreak of war in 1939. After the war Stevens' Garage used these premises (½ mile from their garage) and Enticknap's (see p. 105, lower picture) for a few years, mainly for storage of an ex-WD contract for 100 trucks. After many years the site was cleared, and now two office blocks stand on the site.

Light Parcel Carrier, 1910. This company delivered parcels twice daily on a circuit of Fleet, Bentley, Farnham, Aldershot, Tongham, Farnborough and Cove. The vehicle was an Auto-Carrier, made by AC Cars of London between 1908 and 1912. This Aldershot-based vehicle had a yellow body and rich maroon leather seat. Richard Pool was the agent in Fleet.

Resurfacing the road, 1912. Surfacing the roads was undertaken by the Council, to reduce the complaints of dust in the summer and potholes and ruts in the winter. The tar tank was heated underneath and the liquid tar was pumped through hoses and sprayed on to the road; small chippings were scattered in the tar by shovel and the result was rolled by the steam roller. Laslett's were in the Fleet Road, in the right-hand of the pair of single-storey shops five below today's Gurkha Square car park.

Council dustcart, 1915. This was one of the first dustcarts with fitted covers to keep in the dust and smell. There were two sliding covers each side, not opposite each other. The refuse was tipped in the opening from the zinc bath that two men carried to your dustbin. Much of the rubbish was ash from coal fires, so it was a dirty, dusty job. Up to the end of the war the rubbish was tipped off Pondtail Road, and in later years it built up the common land where Tavistock was built. This view shows the rear of the Council offices from Upper Street.

Parnell's horse and van, 1922. Parnell's had several horse carts: one four-wheeled cart had a large tank to deliver paraffin (used for heating and lighting) all over the district. This van was the boot and shoe vehicle; it would travel to Hartley Wintney and on to Odiham and anywhere else they had a boot repair contract. The repaired boots and shoes would be loaded up in the morning and the van would return in the evening with footwear needing to be cobbled. Parnell's are now accepted as the earliest shop to trade in brick-built premises in Fleet Road. The shops were built in 1880 by Mr Parnell's London builders, who travelled to Fleet daily by train arriving at 7 a.m. They brought some of the lintels from Newgate Prison which they were demolishing at the time, and these were built into the upper floor.

Eales Brothers' coal lorry, 1925. Two brothers, Percy and Leonard, started the haulage firm in the early 1920s from their house in Reading Road, adjacent to St James Road; their yard was behind the house. They were soon appointed parcel agents for the Southern Railway at Fleet and were running two Ford Model T lorries. They lost the contract in 1948 with nationalisation. In the 1920s a platform Model T was purchased and a coal delivery business was built up, with the coal pens in their yard; this side of the business lasted about fifteen years. After the war Percy's three sons came into the business and the two founders retired. The haulage business closed in 1986 when one of the brothers retired.

Pool's horse brake, 1900. Richard Pool, who had a haulage and furniture removal business in Upper Street, introduced the first service for passengers to Aldershot at the turn of the century. The buses were operated as Fleet and Aldershot Omnibus Company from Pool's office near Lloyds Bank. Charlie Vickery was the driver; he expected the customers to walk up the hills on the route.

Warren's coach, 1930. In 1927 Mr Warren of Atbara Road operated Fleet Coaching Co. and he applied for a licence to run a service from Bramshott Golf Club through Fleet to Aldershot. Fleet Council approved but Aldershot refused. The Aldershot and District Co. had a licence (from Aldershot Council) for a Kings Road service. This started a price war, with the 'Traco' putting two 'chasers' on every Warren service. In two years the return fare to Aldershot dropped from 1s 3d to 3d until a frequency agreement was reached. Warren's ten Guy buses were bought out by the 'Traco' in 1936.

J. Wise's pony and trap, 1925. Mr Wise ran a pastrycook and confectionery business in Aldershot Road in the left-hand shop at Pondtail Bridge. The business ran from 1925 until the outbreak of war. He made a name for quality, and regular deliveries were made all over the district.

Mr P. Neal and milk float, 1928. Oakwood Dairy, run by Mr Neal, was in business from 1926 to the 1950s. There were half a dozen 'one man dairies' in the area in the 1930s and '40s but not many survived as long as Neal's. In the early days the cart was fitted with a large churn with a tap and ½ pint and 1 pint measures. The measure was filled from the churn and the milk was tipped into your jug. There were two deliveries a day seven days a week before the war.

Rutter's horse and cart, 1910. Rutter's, on the corner of Victoria and Fleet roads (north side), opened as a high class butcher — both in the quality of the meat and also the speed of delivery of orders to the big houses.

Rutter's errand boy, 1922. Frank Cousins started at 8.30 a.m. daily and finished at 8.30 on Saturday evening. His family lived at Ancells Farm in a tied cottage; his father was in charge of the polo grounds. Frank would make deliveries all morning to the outlying areas with the smaller packets, perhaps 3 or 4 miles away, and would then cycle home for his thirty-minute dinner break.

Fleet Coach, 1949. A new coach with Vincents of Reading bodywork was photographed at a pre-delivery trade fair. The company was founded in 1924 by the William Davieses (father and son) and they started as motor engineers. After the war W.G. Davies started the coach business and it soon became Fleet Coaches; today they run a fleet of a dozen or so luxury coaches.

Two Fleet Coaches and staff, 1955. Jack Welch, mechanic, and drivers Bobby Hunter, Ron Vimpany, Steve Sayers and Jack Rushbridge are shown. The business started in small premises between the Oatsheaf and the police station and today occupies four large garages and an office in the same area. Among the directors today are the two daughters of 'young' Bill Davies.

Fleet station approach, 1927. A Traction Company coach is waiting to start its run back to Aldershot and three taxis are parked in front of the station. A quiet scene, but if you went to the right of the coal trucks there would be a totally different picture with many men unloading the trucks either into pens (adjacent to today's business park) or on to carts; this was all done with shovels or forks, nothing mechanised. The sidings went through to the end of today's car park and there were two tracks in places. Four trains a day, two up and two down, would shunt the trucks, collect the empties and place the full ones in their correct place in the yard. The goods yard closed in 1969.

Fleet station, 1906. A fine view of the entrance to the platforms that was built when the tracks were upgraded from two to four lines in 1904. On the other side of Station Bridge, where the original Fleet Pond station had been built, there was a siding against the golf course where half a dozen coal trucks were left for the pump house, which provided air for the electro-pneumatic signal system. Air for the system between Brookwood and Worting was provided here. In the late 1950s the steam engine was changed to an electric motor but in 1966, on electrification, a new system was installed and the pump house etc. was demolished.

Fleet station, 1925. The photographer is standing on the Up platform looking towards Station Bridge with an express approaching. At the end of the platform by the bridge was the stationmaster's house; there was one at each station until the 1950s. Today the gate on to the platform can still be seen in the iron railings, while the site of the house is now part of the car park. The building on the left behind the Down platform is the parcel shed, which held three box wagons. This is where Eales Bros collected parcels for delivery around the district.

Bramshott Halt, 1950s. A Schools class locomotive is passing through the Halt on its way to Basingstoke. The Halt was opened just after the golf club started in 1905 when motor cars were not common and closed in the 1950s. In the last few years before it closed three or four trains a day would stop if a request was made in advance to Fleet or Farnborough station. In the late 1940s and '50s the army built a petrol storage facility at what was later to become Fleet Pond picnic area, and a siding was run alongside the normal lines to this area for the tanker wagons to be discharged.

CHAPTER SEVEN

SPORT

A vintage De Dion, 1930s. The Stevens brothers were in the motor business almost from the introduction of the motor car. They were often called to Ewshot Hall where Col. Wilkes had a motor car. Soon Lord Calthorpe and Dr Frere (a local GP and benefactor) bought cars from Stevens Bros. In the 1930s and '40s there was often a 1904 De Dion in the showroom; this was entered in the London to Brighton run. Here Redvers Stevens is seen with Syd Farr navigating.

Crookham Football Club, 1897. Various grounds were used by the club over the years including a site close to Coxheath Bridge, but in the 1930s they moved to Abercorn playing fields opposite the Wyvern. They joined the Aldershot League as soon as it was founded and moved up and down the divisions for many years. This team comprised E. Potter, H. Griffin, S. Griffin, ? Jenkins, ? Dempster, F. Rydon, R. Sisterton, F. Bloor, J. King, A. White, E. Simms, W. Wake and W. Goddard.

Fleet Wednesday football team, *c.* 1905. Until the late 1960s most shops closed at 1 p.m. on Wednesday afternoons to enable the staff to work on the other five and a half days in the week (excluding Sunday). 'Wednesday' football and cricket teams were generally made up of shop staff who could not play on Saturdays. This team, which played in the Aldershot Wednesday League, was G. Vass, H. Hodder, H. Sayers, F. Love, J. Long, H. Tocock, W. Stacey, J. Bowerman, F. Fround (captain), J. Carter and A. Oakley, with F. Parker (referee, a newsagent) and P. Harden (linesman, a butcher).

Fleet football team, 1950. After the war Fleet played in the Aldershot League at their ground in Crookham Road opposite Glen Road. In the 1960s they became more ambitious and joined the stronger Basingstoke League. This team comprised H. Pearce, D. Stacey, R. Sawyer, G. Hill, D. Powell, J. Byrne, D. Gardiner, R. Goodsell, S. Brown (captain), J. Brooks and S. Sayers. The colours from the '20s (at least) were light and dark blue. The club will celebrate its centenary in a couple of years' time.

Hunt meeting at the Oatsheaf, 1905. Mr Chinnock of Dinorben Court owned a pack of fox hounds and often brought them to the Oatsheaf for the meet. There was very little danger in having forty or so dogs and horses running along the road at this time. They invariably hunted over the Calthorpe estate.

Fleet Ladies' Hockey Team, 1928/9. The ladies' section of the Hockey Club played twenty-seven matches in this season with teams from as far away as Basingstoke, Godalming, Byfleet and Reading. Miss M. Pidwell was the captain. Matches were played on the side of the cricket field, alternating with the men's team. Dr Frere was the Club President.

Fleet Men's Hockey Team, 1927/8. The men's section played twenty-seven matches in their black and orange strip with teams from as far away as Woking and Basingstoke. The club was formed in 1925 and is still in existence today, playing on the same ground. Transport to away matches was provided by Mr Hankins with one of his covered lorries, and his invoice for all the away games in this season was for £7 13s 4d.

Motor-cycle Club Meeting, 1922. The Fleet and Crookham Club often met at the Oatsheaf for social meetings and when they went on a run. The machines in those days were smaller and less reliable, and the club would organise navigation and reliability runs – often at night. As can be seen there was a range of machines, solo and with sidecars, and even light cars.

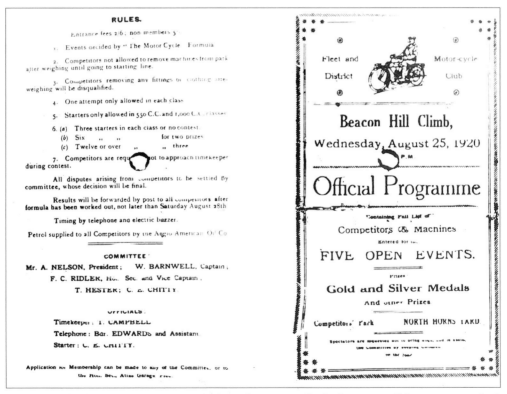

Motor-cycle Club programme, 1920. The annual Beacon Hill Climb was a well-known event which attracted entries from a wide area. The idea was to climb the hill (a rough track on Army ground) in the fastest time, and often just to get to the top was an achievement. The secretary was Mr Ridler, the one-time owner of the Atlas Garage in Fleet Road; he was building two-stroke and four-stroke motor-cycles. The other committee members were no mean riders and mechanics.

Fleet Cricket Club, 1929. Matches were played at The Beeches, owned by Mr Bloore, until he sold the property and the North Hants Golf Club was laid out. Matches were then played on the field by Birch Avenue until the Cricket Club was founded, and Lord Calthorpe gave a piece of ground in Reading Road at a cost of £5 a year. The club, founded in the first few years of this century, still plays on the same ground. The event pictured is the annual 'married versus single'.

Crookham Cricket Club, 1904. Cricket was played in Crookham near Chequers Bridge as early as the 1890s, and by the 1920s matches were played near the Wyvern; but the Fleet club with its better ground and facilities brought about the demise of the village team. The Rev. W.J. Wickham, long-time vicar of Crookham, is shown wearing a boater.

Bramshott Golf Club, 1908. Entrance to the club was opposite Bramshott Bridge off Cove Road. The course was opened in 1904, having been laid out by J.H. Taylor, an open champion, and was 'one of the finest inland courses in the kingdom'. The captain in 1910 was the current *News of the World* match play champion, Tom Ball. By 1920 a two-storey clubhouse had been built with twenty-three bedrooms and the old clubhouse had been given over to the ladies. Bramshott Halt railway station was opened 100 yards from the clubhouse. It was an 18-hole 6,020 yard course with 200 members when it closed in 1939. Harry Varden held the professional record with 73.

North Hants Golf Club, 1912. The clubhouse and grounds on the Minley Road were The Beeches, owned by Mr Bloore – an affluent London timber merchant. The remainder of the course towards Elvetham belongs to Lord Calthorpe. The 18-hole course is 6,020 yards long and before the war there were tennis courts and croquet lawns set in beautiful surroundings. The Elvetham Estates still own three-quarters of the course, and with the coming of the adjacent Railroad Heath development, rearrangement of a few holes will have to be made.

Polo match, 1926. The Wellington Polo Club's ground was attached to Ancells Farm in Cove Road and stretched up to Brook House. The grounds were close to the Minley Road and the derelict pavilion was demolished when the M3 was built. In the playing season (March to September) three meetings a week were held, plus four tournament weeks. There were three playing pitches, one being reserved for the ladies, and a practice pitch.

Indian grooms and the stables, 1926. Invariably an overseas team would be guests of the owner of Ancells Farm for at least one of the tournaments, and opponents would be invited by the Wellington Club to play the guests who would tour in this country for the season. The grooms lived in the tack rooms.

Jim Heanes. Born in Salisbury, he moved to Fleet when he married in the 1920s. Before the war he was a keen trialist and scrambler riding Ariel and Matchless machines, whose factories gave him support. After the war he opened a garage with Jack Foster, another keen motorcyclist, in Crookham village, later moving to Dogmersfield where Foster and Heanes (under new ownership) can still be seen. His hobby was restoring old motor-cycles and showing them at historic machine events at home and abroad.

Ken Heanes. Ken was fortunate to be apprenticed to Archers of Aldershot (another famous motor-cycling family). He first competed at the age of twelve, gaining a trophy in an event at Hartley Wintney, and last rode at occasional events at sixty-three – fifty years in the saddle. He rode in trials and scrambles (now moto cross), gaining over 300 awards, including the '100 mile scramble' trophy on three occasions. He became a member of the British team to ride in the Olympics of motor-cycling (ISDT) in seventeen consecutive events, gaining ten gold and three silver medals. Having ridden all over Europe and the USA, he retired from riding in 1971 and became British team manager until 1975.

Holland Birkett. After buying 3 Pondtail Road, a workshop/garage was added to enable 'Holley' to pursue his hobby of tuning and modifying his Austin 7 to get better petrol consumption in order to eke out his wartime ration. With the end of the war Austin 7s and Bugattis were stripped, rebuilt and sold on to provide funds for his passion of competing in night navigation rallies, time trials and economy runs. He is here pictured at Hindhead on a night run. 'Holley' was instrumental in founding the 750 Club, the Veteran Sports Car Club and the Hants and Berks Motor Club, all of which are still in existence. He gave a creditable performance when he competed in the Monte Carlo Rally on several occasions, and his name is still perpetuated in the 'Birkett 6 hour race' at Snetterton.

No. 3 Pondtail Road, 1943. In 1910 the building was a hand laundry and by 1929 it was a dogs' hospital. Holland Birkett took over in 1941 as the resident vet and used the old laundry as a surgery and as a home. In the early days his wife Joan partitioned the building to provide rooms for the family, which soon included two daughters. As well as helping in the surgery and looking after the kennels Joan became a very successful breeder of Pyrenean Mountain dogs. They left Pondtail in 1964 after Holley and his third wife were tragically killed in a light plane crash.

Cycle Speedway, 1949. The original track was laid out in the Firs Meadow, which is where the police station was built in 1967. Friendly matches were held on Sunday afternoons and attracted a crowd of two or three hundred. Ian Hester is leading this race, at one of the first meetings.

Cycle Speedway Track, 1952. In 1951 Fleet Council leased the club a piece of ground behind the cricket field, where the pitch and putt course is today. With the help of friends and parents the area was cleared of bushes and laid out as a 300 yard circuit with an electrically operated starting gate, cinder track and safety fencing. The inaugural meeting was screened by BBC (South) TV and the Fleet Falcons rode against the Stoughton Greyhounds. In 1954 one of the semi-finals of the British Riders Championship was held on this track. The Falcons could boast 500–600 spectators at each meeting.

Tug of War team, 1941. The Fleet Civil Defence team are competing in their first competition during War Weapons Week. The team was, back row: H. Vickery, J. Cox, W. Hook, G. Longhurst, T. Godfrey, B. Belcher, H. Silver; front row: S. Scoffield, W. Barton, -?-, and S. Culver. Transport during the war was by cycle, and the team and their supporters often appeared at Guildford, Woking and Basingstoke. After the war the club was renamed Fleet and in 1946 took part in the AAA Championships at White City; they were still pulling well in the late 1950s.

Moto Ball, 1949. The game was played by members of various motor-cycle clubs, and this was a match between Fleet and Basingstoke. The sport was very popular between the 1930s and the 1950s with the only requirement for a pitch being a fairly flat field with grass. Matches were held on several occasions on The Views in Carnival Week. Home games were played at Causeway Farm, Goddards Farm or Queen Elizabeth Barracks. Away matches were played as far off as Cheltenham, Bolton, Ipswich, Maldon and South Molton.

CHAPTER EIGHT

INDUSTRY

Pool's timber yard, 1902. Mr Herbert Pool moved from the Oatsheaf area along Fleet Road towards the northern entrance of the Hart Centre. Across the road, above the property adjacent to the old post office, can still be seen the ornamental P & S (for Pool and Son): the whole of this block was used for offices with builder's yard and joinery works behind. The old wooden Priory was the stables. Across the road were the sawmills, which in the First World War had a large contract to supply timber to the War Office. The rails on which the bed, or track, ran were discovered under the floors of the two shops demolished in 1989.

Liming's Garage, 1903. This garage in Aldershot Road was on the site of the present garage opposite The Verne. The Limings were a large well-known family who had lived in Crookham for at least 300 years and could at times boast a policeman, publican, schoolmaster, builder and sailor. The car is a 1901 or 1902 Coventry-built MMC which cost 350 guineas, and the motor-cycle in the centre is probably a Birmingham-built 2¼ h.p. Quadrant costing 42 guineas.

Atlas Motor and Cycle Works, 1920. Built in the early years of the century for Mr George Kennedy, this garage was just below the site of Gurkha Square car park and remained a garage until 1936. The side and rear walls remain but the frontage is now three shops. By 1909 it was Halimote Garage, leased to the Aldershot and District Traction Co. as motor engineers. By 1919 Mr Ridler owned the Atlas Works where he built two- and four-stroke motor-cycles and repaired cars, including the Model T shown here, no doubt. From 1919 to 1935 Stevens Bros were in residence; in the latter year the garage closed.

King and Bartlett, 1904. The premises to the left were in use in the 1820s and were the original site of worship in Fleet. In 1922 a large table top was still in the workshop: it was said to be where dissenters sat around the table to talk and read the Bible. Tom King started his coachbuilder's business here in 1905, building any type of horse-drawn carriage or 'special' as required. Mr Bartlett only remained his partner for about ten years. The business closed in the late 1920s and Mr Davies took over. The two-storey building is adjacent to the property next to St James Road in Crookham Road.

Enticknap's Garage, 1925. Mr P.J. Enticknap built his garage in Crookham Road adjacent to Coxheath Road in 1922, and being the only garage in that area business was always brisk and he stayed there for ten years until Mr Welch took over. After the war Stevens used the building as a store for several years before a block of flats was built on the corner. The make of the motor-cycle is unknown but the car on the left is a 1915 Model T Ford. On the right is another Model T, a 1925 van belonging to Mr Irvine – whose bakery was along the road opposite The Lea.

Stevens' Garage, 1930. Mr Stevens chose a prime site along Fleet Road to set his five sons up in business, and opened here in 1902 when he foresaw that the motor car was going to be big business. Two of his sons became proficient at starting and maintaining Col. Wilkes' (of Ewshot Hall) Rover car. A telephone call would have the two lads dashing off on their bikes to get the car working. Two of Col. Wilkes' sons had moved to Birmingham, designed the Rover and gave the first one to their father. Stevens were soon appointed distributors for Rovers and today their successors (now in Albert Street) still hold the franchise. Fleet's ambulance (driven by Stevens staff) was parked in the open-fronted building to the right of the showroom.

Royal Dairy milk float, c. 1930. The coachbuilding side of Stevens' business was carried out in a two-bay brick building in Albert Street. In the early 1930s Stevens produced this float to a new design: rubber tyres, three wheels for a smoother ride and the driver partially sheltered from the weather. They built hundreds before horse-drawn was replaced by electric after the war. This dairy was in the Fleet Road opposite what is now Gurkha Square car park from 1907 until the 1940s.

Horse-drawn carts, *c.* 1923. A selection of floats, traps and waggons are lined up in Albert Street outside the wheelwrights and farriers area that Stevens occupied from the Hart Centre north entrance along towards Church Road to the two grey stone panelled shops in Fleet Road. The whole block went through to Albert Street. Paint shops for cars and the wooden vehicles were all in this road. These buildings disappeared when Stevens closed in 1967, and gradually County Commercial Cars spread along Albert Street up to the roadway by the garage.

Milk floats at the station, 1935. At the Farnborough end behind the Up platform there was a 'roll on roll off' siding where Stevens' milk floats were loaded on to 'flats' for delivery. Hundreds of floats for Express and United Dairies were sent up to London from the station over the years. In the 1950s and '60s County tractors were also sent from this siding.

County six-wheeled truck, 1930. County Commercial Cars came to Fleet in 1929 when the company was formed, and used Pool's old steam engine shed at 127 Albert Street. In the early days a new Ford four-wheeled truck was converted to a longer six-wheeled model. After a few years County supplied Ford at Dagenham with springs, a centre axle and various other special parts, and the six-wheeler was built on the Ford assembly line at Dagenham. This view shows an early vehicle outside 127 Albert Street, and the shop on the left is on the corner of Upper Street. During the war every barrage balloon (land-based) was attached to one of these six-wheelers.

High clearance vehicle, 1946. After the war County set about finding a new product and they soon obtained an order for six 4 ft high clearance vehicles based on WD surplus Ford War Office Trucks No. 6 vehicles to spray blackcurrant bushes. Next came an order for two similar vehicles but with 7 ft clearance (shown here) for spraying cordon (single-stemmed) apple trees. The biggest problem in those days was obtaining materials: large diameter tubes, steel plate, large tyres and wheels, etc.

Crawler tractor, 1947. County next received an order from a pest control company for five narrow-track tractors for carrying spray equipment between apple trees and in hop gardens. Evaluation was carried out at the same time on a wider (52½ in gauge) machine and this was the resulting tractor, which continued in production until 1967. Thousands were built over the years and at one time in the mid-1950s there was an additional assembly line at Longparish near Andover: forty to forty-five were built each week. The original had a 29 h.p. engine and cost £795.

County 1884, 1982. This 188 h.p. four wheel drive was the most powerful and last tractor introduced by County Tractors (as the company was now known) before they went into receivership in 1983. Four-wheel-drive tractors had been manufactured from 1958 and were sold all over the world with hundreds of different pieces of equipment mounted on the basic machine. Drilling rigs, cranes, welding equipment, cement mixers, tipper bodies, winches, scrapers, dozers and fifth wheel couplings were just some of the accessories. This year (1998) being the fiftieth anniversary of the first production machines, there was a large 'Tracks Across the Field' club event, at which many County tractors came back to Hampshire and did a weekend's work.

Marsh Laundry staff party, 1948. The staff are in their decorated canteen with the owners Mr and Mrs Marsh, possibly about to enjoy the Christmas entertainment. The laundry occupied part of Richard Pool's site from Fleet Road (a small shop) through to Albert Street along Upper Street. The business opened in 1943 and soon had a contract for many of the service units from as far as 40 miles around. By 1947 the number of service personnel had decreased and the laundry's three vans were collecting from private houses to keep the staff of eighty busy, but the laundry joined with the Royal Herts Laundry in 1949 and the Fleet site was closed.

The Art Laundry, 1935. This laundry was in Kenilworth Road on the Avondale Road corner, and was in business from 1926 until the outbreak of war. Their 1935 Silver Jubilee decorations were spectacular for a small concern, with flags and bunting and floodlighting of the building at night. During the war Huntley and Palmer, the Reading biscuit manufacturers, used the building as an outstation; local girls were enlisted to pack the biscuits for 'war work'. There was another of these outstations in Sandy Lane, Crookham. After the war Dae Health Laboratory used the premises for the packing and despatch of Valderma Cream. The premises were demolished in the 1960s and houses now stand on the site.

North Hants Tyre and Remoulding Co. Ltd, 1948. Opened in 1948 by John Pettifor, the firm started in a small corrugated-iron workshop in Fleet Road close to the Station (now Links) Hotel. At the time remoulds were seen to be good cheap tyre replacements for the average car. The premises were soon enlarged, as remoulds became more popular.

North Hants Tyre and Remoulding Co. Ltd display, mid-1950s. This display was mounted in the marquee at the Fleet Carnival Trade Fair. Stan Burton, the Sales Manager, is in attendance. Eventually, as remoulds became more complex as the speed of cars increased, the company became agents for foreign tyres and wheels. The business moved along the Fleet Road to the junction of Avondale Road.

Terrace Garage, 1933. The garage is in Fleet Road adjacent to Avondale Parade; here a new 33 C/S Matchless motor-cycle is on the forecourt. The opening to the left is today an entrance to the industrial premises behind. The building was erected for Mr Barnwell after the First World War and his motor works carried on until 1933 when Mr Langford took over. For several years the garage has been associated with the used cars next door.

Ken Heanes Ltd, 1980. In 1955 the business started in Reading Road, close to Clarence Road, in a corrugated-iron shed. By adding adjoining properties and rebuilding, a smart showroom and workshop emerged. For many years only British machines were sold but gradually Japanese and other foreign makes crept in. Ken sponsored Eddie Kidd and built the machine for his record jump over fourteen double-decker buses.

CHAPTER NINE

PUBLIC HALLS AND HOUSES

Pinewood Hall, 1904. The Hall and Pearson's office block were built on the Fleet and Kings roads corner in 1903. The Hall was built as a furniture depository, although it was used in its early years as an auction room. In 1908 Mr Pearson was persuaded by some of his friends to allow the building to be used as a concert hall, as they said Weber's Theatre was a 'flea pit'. A stage was erected, and when an event was imminent the gentry's coachmen would collect chairs from the local churches and set them up in the hall, returning them the next morning. When Weber's Theatre was burnt to the ground Pinewood Hall became the public hall.

Fire at Weber's Theatre, 1914. The wooden theatre had stood for several years between Church Road and Birch Avenue in front of the present telephone exchange, and with its large stage it was a fine setting for drama evenings. It was obviously becoming dilapidated, however. The fact that it was a wooden building, together with the firemen's turn-out time, which was fifteen minutes, guaranteed that this would be the resulting picture.

New Hall, 1936. After 1918 two Army surplus corrugated-iron buildings were bought and erected side by side, with wooden panelling on the inside. Heating was by a couple of 'slow but sure' stoves, but when the audience arrived the hall soon became comfortable. The main hall had a stage and a large floor area, while the smaller hall had a good-size kitchen and serving area plus a large space that could be laid out for meals. Both floors were marked out as badminton courts. The hall was open most days for dances, plays, concerts, whist drives, etc. Fleet Mothers' Union met here monthly. The buildings on the left are the bakehouse and outbuildings of Voller's the bakers; some of the buildings are still standing.

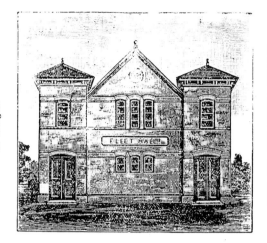

The Fleet Hall.

The above hall is carried on by the Fleet Hall Company, Limited, consisting of share-holders holding 650 fully paid-up shares of £1 each.

Directors:—Mr. J. Oakley, Chairman, Miss L. Henslow, Miss I. Foulger, W. Bloore, Esq. Rev. C. O. Munns, Messrs. Ivor Smith and J. Morgan.

Architect:—Mr. F. F. Husted. Builders:—Messrs. Pool and Sons.

Opened in 1891.

Secretary: Mr. Geo. Hill, South View, Albert Street, to whom all communications respecting the hire of the hall, etc., should be addressed.

Fleet Hall trade card, 1902. The hall was on the east side of Fleet Road 100 yards above Upper Street; the site today has one large and four smaller shops with a layby. This was a lecture and concert hall when it was opened in 1891, having been built by Pool and Son. With the coming of the early (silent) films a two-year trial began, using battery electric power and a carbon light beam to project the film. A skilled pianist accompanied the scenes with appropriate music. A Saturday matinée, with the children walking up to 5 miles from outlying villages, was very popular. The Chairman of Directors was Mr J. Oakley. The hall was demolished in 1924.

Fleet Road and Biograph, Fleet.

Fleet Biograph, 1921. The Biograph was the original Fleet Hall (on the right next to the chemist) and changed its name when it was converted to a full-time cinema. This was the policy of the new owner Mr Watmore, and as soon as the talkies arrived it proved a very good move.

Guard of Honour, 1928. The refurbished Biograph was reopened as The Palladium in 1928 and the Guard of Honour was no doubt recruited from a local dancing school. The following year Mr Watmore sold out to County Cinemas, which was headed by Mr C. Donado – an entrepreneur from Guildford Road. Within a year the name had been changed to King George's Cinema, and in 1936 the building was being enlarged with a restyled foyer.

Odeon Cinema, 1951. It was opened in November 1937 as the County Cinema by Florence Desmond, whose films were often shown here. By now the shop to the right had become a café, sweets and cigarette shop, and within a few years it was part of the cinema complex. At the beginning of the war the County group had sold out to the larger Odeon group who renamed the cinema. Odeon remained the last name and owner, because in 1957 it finally closed, beaten by television.

Laying the foundation stone of the Institute, Reading Room and Gymnasium in Albert Street, 1926. The building was almost opposite today's Hart Centre car park entrance, and was built before the turn of the century. It was given by Col. Horniblow, owner of The Views and one of Fleet's biggest benefactors, as a memorial to Queen Victoria. With the loss of Fleet Hall for meetings, concerts, etc. (it was by now a cinema) another hall was required, and in 1926 the Church decided to build a new larger building on the site. The foundation stone was laid in November 1926 by Edgar Figgis of Courtmoor House, seen here with the Vicar Wilson Pearce and Fred Snuggs (on the right), the builder. The stone is now in the end of Victoria Court, the block of flats eventually built on the site.

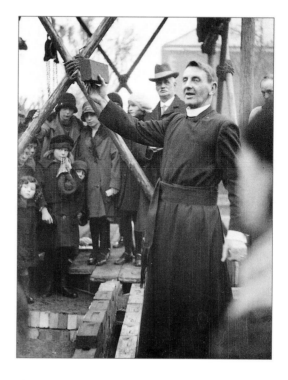

Selling bricks, 1926. The new Institute was built by public subscription and hundreds of bricks were bought by the public for 6d each. The hall was let for many functions including concerts, dances, whist drives, horticultural shows, pantomimes, gang shows, blood transfusion, mother and baby clinics, and plays. The Vicar Wilson Pearce is seen here selling bricks on the day the foundation stone was laid. With the increase in population and in the age of the hall it was a great relief when in 1973 the Assembly Halls (now the Harlington Centre) were opened, and the Institute was demolished.

Air Rifle Club, 1909/10. There were two air rifle clubs in Fleet at this time, one based at the Institute and the other at Fleet Club (now the British Legion) in Clarence Road. There was also a rifle club in Fleet with a range behind the Oatsheaf towards the cricket ground; another club at Crookham used an army range near the Wyvern. Both air rifle and full-bore rifle shooting were very popular at this time, with ranges open several times a week for matches or practice shooting.

Choir and orchestra, 1934. The annual concert given by George Hodkin and his orchestra and choir was one of the highlights of the year in the Institute. The show this year was *Merrie England*, given with pianist Miss H. Caley. The capacity audience was always appreciative of the performance. Mr G. Hodkin was headmaster of Crookham School from 1931 until 1950.

Fleet Boys' Club Annual Social, 1936. The Boys' Club Social was a grand affair with all the boys smartly dressed. The boys had use of the hall three nights a week; various games, including billiards (two tables) and table tennis, discussions and lectures were provided. Charlie Roe from the Reading Road photographers was a long-time leader.

Church pantomime, 1952. For many years the Church staged a pantomime in the Institute after Christmas. Many members appeared year after year, proving that they were willing to give the audience a good laugh at their expense. A pantomime is still part of the Church's Christmas festivities, with the show now being held in SS Philip and James' church hall.

Dr Falkland Cary. Born in County Kildare in 1897, he was educated at Trinity College Medical School, Dublin. He took a break in studies to join the Royal Navy during the First World War. On qualifying he joined a Harrogate practice, which he later headed. Here he found some time for amateur dramatics, playwriting and production. Dr Cary moved to Fleet in 1944 and soon found there was no amateur dramatic society. He soon had a card in the window of most shops and at the first meeting seventy-five people turned up, with most of them joining to form Fleet Players. The Institute, which by now was the church hall, seated over 200 and had a large stage, and for about twenty-five years all the plays (usually three a year) were performed here, before the Assembly Halls were opened. Dr Cary always found time to bring his West End and professional experience to the local players. He wrote and collaborated in more than sixty plays including *Sailor Beware*, *Watch it Sailor*, *Rock-a-bye Sailor*, *Big Bad Mouse* and *Madam Tic-Tac*. Philip Weathers and Philip King were two of his co-authors. Dr Cary also wrote novels with A.A. Thomson and a handbook on play writing. He lived in a large house close to the junction of Kings and Fleet roads. He had a very large model railway layout in a converted stable to which many guests were invited to 'run trains at Irish Railways'. Dr Cary died in April 1989.

The Queens Head, 1896. Situated on the island at the junction of Pilcot Hill, Chatter Alley and Church Lane at Dogsmerfield, it would have been built some sixty years earlier to serve the local farm labourers. Being on an island site and in a conservation area, the pub has kept much of its original charm. May's Brewery was in Basingstoke and in the brewery upheaval after the war it was bought out by Simmonds of Reading.

The Chequers Inn, 1929. Situated in the Crondall Road out of Crookham village, close to the canal, it is an eighteenth-century building which has had close associations with the canal. It was awarded the first contract for boarding canal employees and horses used for towing barges along the canal tow-path. Canal Cottage over Chequers Bridge is believed to have been the office of the original canal company that traded from 1794.

Wyvern Arms, 1928. The Wyvern was opened in the 1860s, having been built by Mr Maxwell Lefroy. A wyvern is a winged mythical creature with two legs, and is also the emblem of the Crondall Lefroy family. The building of a public house by Mr Lefroy must have raised a few eyebrows, as he was supporting Crondall and Dogsmerfield churches and he had just built churches at Crookham and Fleet.

Crookham Street Social Club, 1909. The club was built on Mr White's farmland in Crookham Street and stands 100 yards down the road from the Black Horse. Most of the cash to build the club came from local benefactors. In the 1950s, with the relaxing of the betting laws to allow gaming machines (one arm bandits), the club soon had sufficient funds to build a two-storey building on the site. The club is still thriving today.

The Fox and Hounds, 1947. Along Crookham Road backing on to the canal, this inn was built in the early years of the nineteenth century and was a welcome stop to rest and refresh the crews of the barges going up and down the 37-mile canal. In 1838 (the busiest year) the total tonnage passing on to and out of the Wey Navigation (near Weybridge) was 33,879; there is no indication of loads carried, say, from Odiham to Ash, but many barges passed each day. Fox and Hounds landlords through the years have always known how to make extra revenue from the 'back gate'.

The Oatsheaf Hotel, 1906. Crookham Common, part of the Great Heath, was traversed for hundreds of years by merchants on horseback or later in horse-drawn coaches, as Reading Road was the track from Reading to Farnham and the Crookham, Fleet and Minley roads connected the farms of Crookham to the Fleet Mill and beyond to the Hartfordbridge Flats. What better place to put a hotel in the early 1840s than on this busy crossroads? With the growth of Fleet from the 1850s the hotel prospered, but outwardly it is the same today as when it was built.

Broadway Club outing, 1933. One of Warren's coaches, parked by the old Council Offices in Albert Street (close to Upper Street) is ready for a seaside outing to Bognor or Southsea. The Broadway Club opened in the Broadway in Kings Road in about 1908, and by 1933 fine premises had been built behind two houses in Albert Street. The club is now brick built and has been extended several times. It offers fine facilities for its members.

Lismoyne Hotel, 1932. This was the year in which it opened in Church Road opposite Lismoyne Close. The hotel, approached by a winding rhododendron-lined drive, was enlarged in 1970 when a block of bedrooms was added behind the house to the left, the catering area was enlarged and the function room was built. The hotel was converted from Lismoyne, a large house built in the 1880s, one of several in the area built at the same time.

The Station Hotel, 1915. In 1880 Mr Brown of Bracknell built the hotel by the two-track Fleet Pond station, with large stables and a yard. A bowling green and a tennis court were provided. As this trade card shows Mr Wallbank was catering for a sporting clientele. The horse and motor cabs belonged, no doubt, to Mr Kimber, who used the ground along Fleet Road from Kings and Avondale roads to break and graze horses. Road widening and straightening of Minley Road up to Station Bridge meant that the hotel grounds have become very much smaller.

Station Hotel outing, c. 1932. Every year Mr Dodds the landlord (third from the right, with the bow tie) would organise a trip to Bognor or Southsea using the local coaches from Warren's of Sandy Lane. This view on the beach only shows the men, as no doubt the ladies were left at home while the men enjoyed themselves. Mr Cousins, on the left in a cap, worked for many years on the Elvetham Estate before going to Ancells Farm in 1926 when the Polo Grounds were without a groundsman. He had several men under him during the summers when the matches were played.

ACKNOWLEDGEMENTS

I would like to thank the following individuals and organisations, without whose assistance the book would not have been possible.

Mr and Mrs R. Allen, G. Baker, G. Barson, Mrs E. Beale, Mrs E. Bell, Mrs V. Birkett, T. Black, W. Boulter, S. Butt, V. Carr, Mrs G. Cousins, Mrs Q. Davies, B. Dove, E. Eales, R. Eales, Mrs E. Field, A. Fitzpatrick, Hampshire Regiment Museum, Mrs D. Hannawin, K. Heanes, Mrs C. Heathers, I. Hester, P. Holmes, S. Knight, Miss J. Marsh, J. Mill, National Motor Museum, J. Pettifor, RAMC Museum, M. Rich, Mrs M. Roe, Mrs E. Ruffle, J. Rushbridge, Mr and Mrs G. Shaw, D. Small, D. Tapp, D. White.

Although there are over 200 photographs in this book I am sure that there are many more tucked into old cupboards or drawers somewhere in Fleet. If this encourages people to search out their old photographs and allow them to be reproduced there could be a second selection! It would be very sad if such items of interest were to be mistakenly consigned to the bin or a bonfire and lost forever.

Every effort has been made to establish copyright and permission has been sought to reproduce material where appropriate.

LIST OF ILLUSTRATIONS